True Loving, Jordi Bernadó

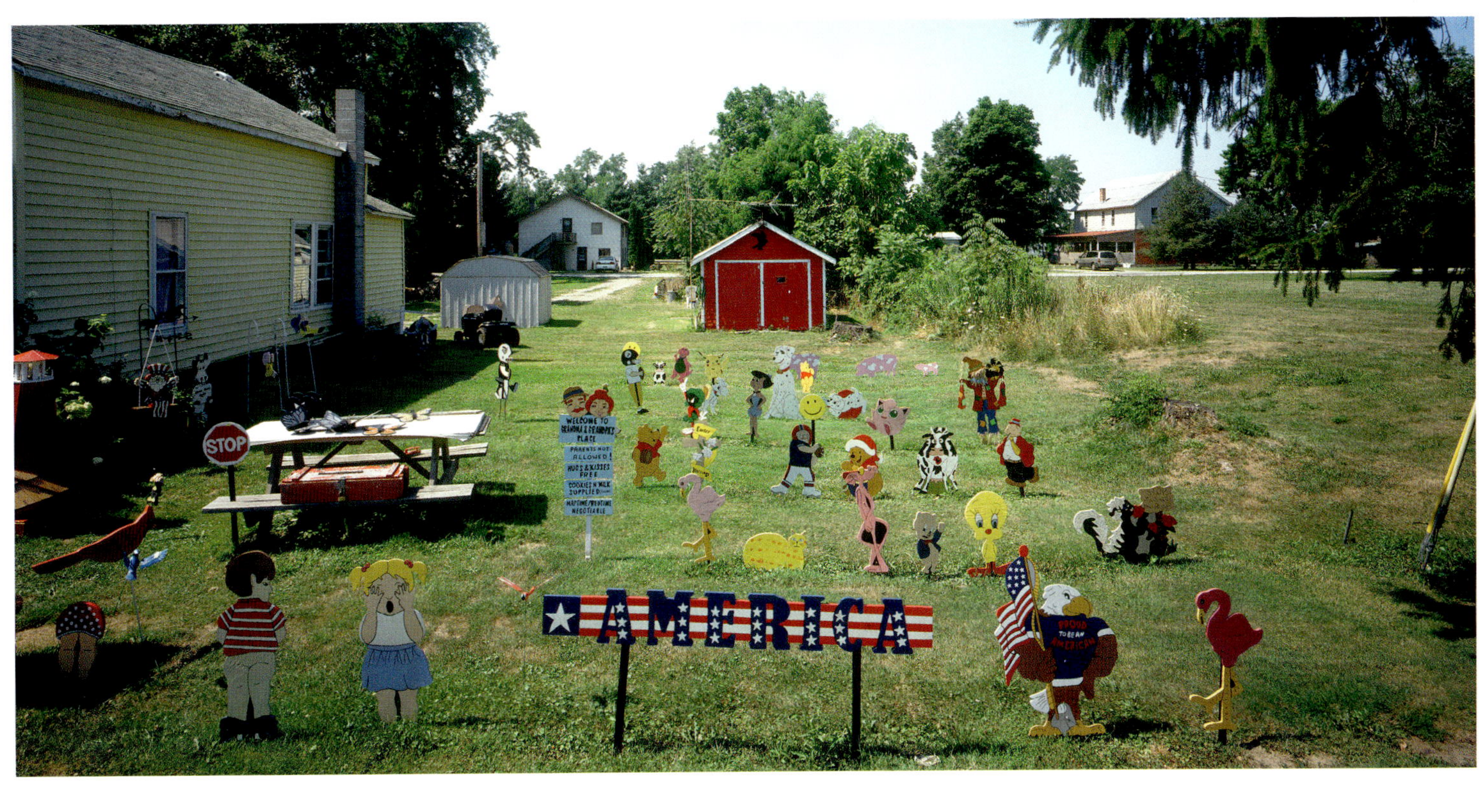

Barcelona, New York

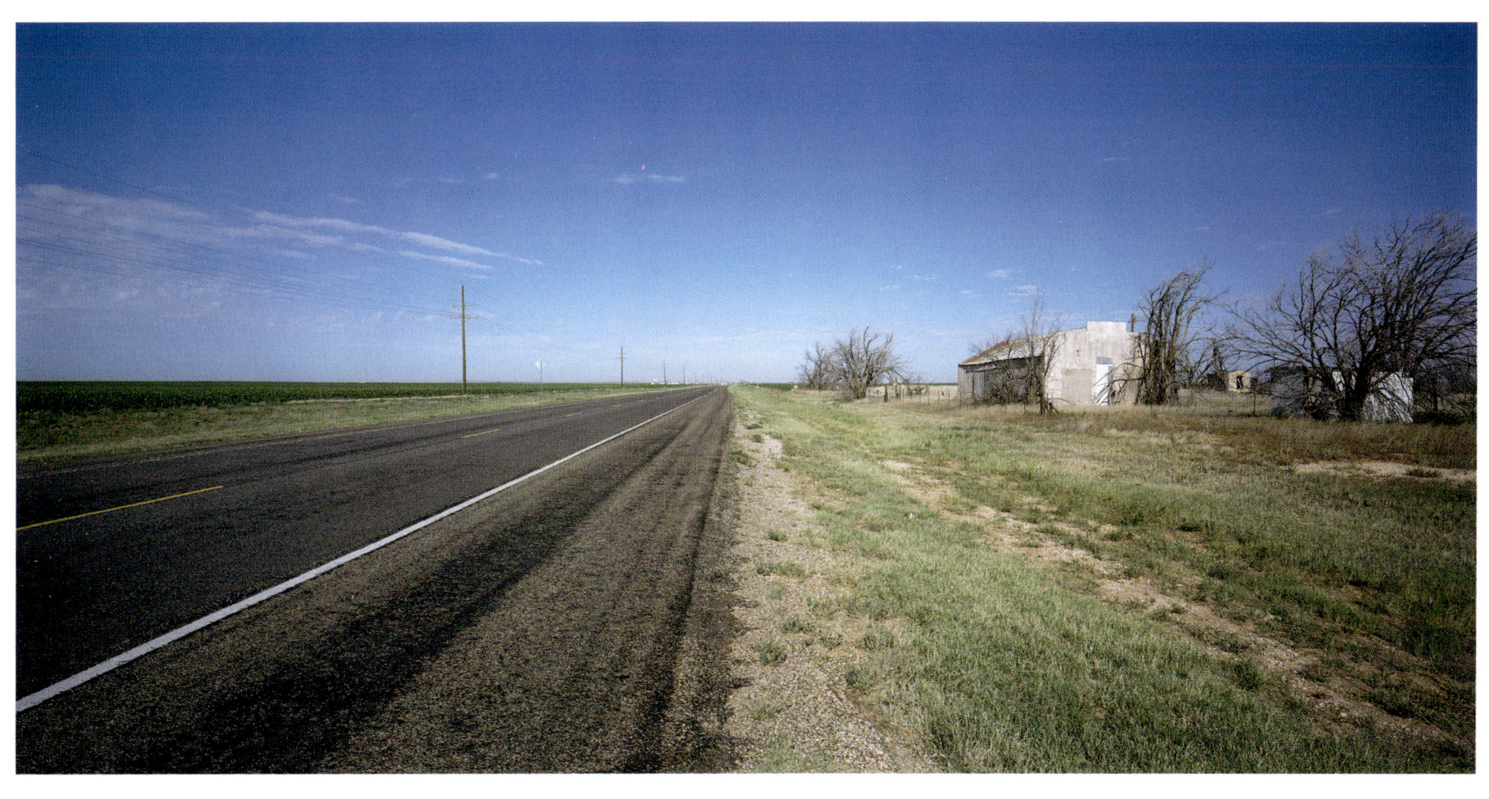

Tokyo, Texas

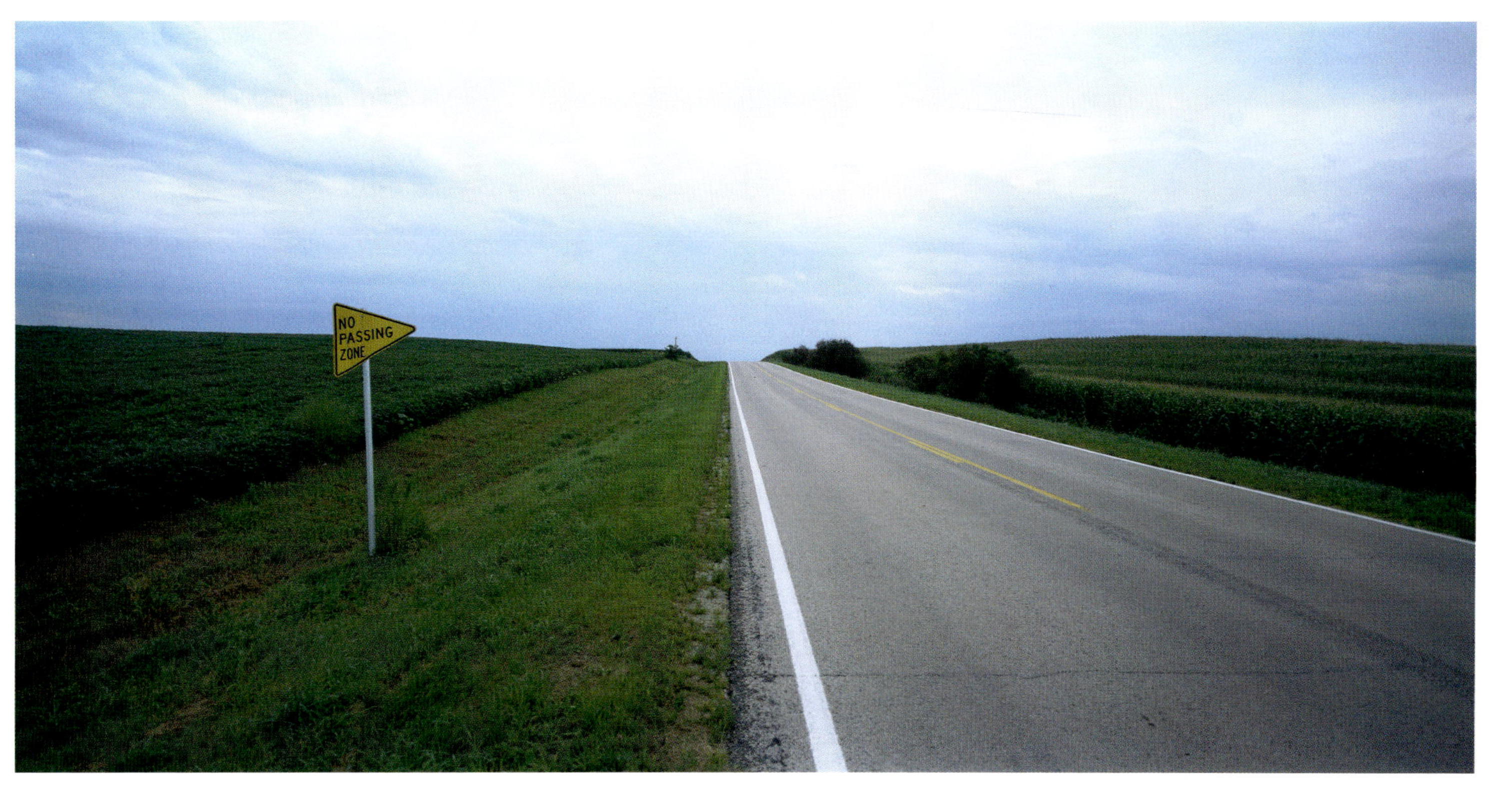

Eden, Illinois

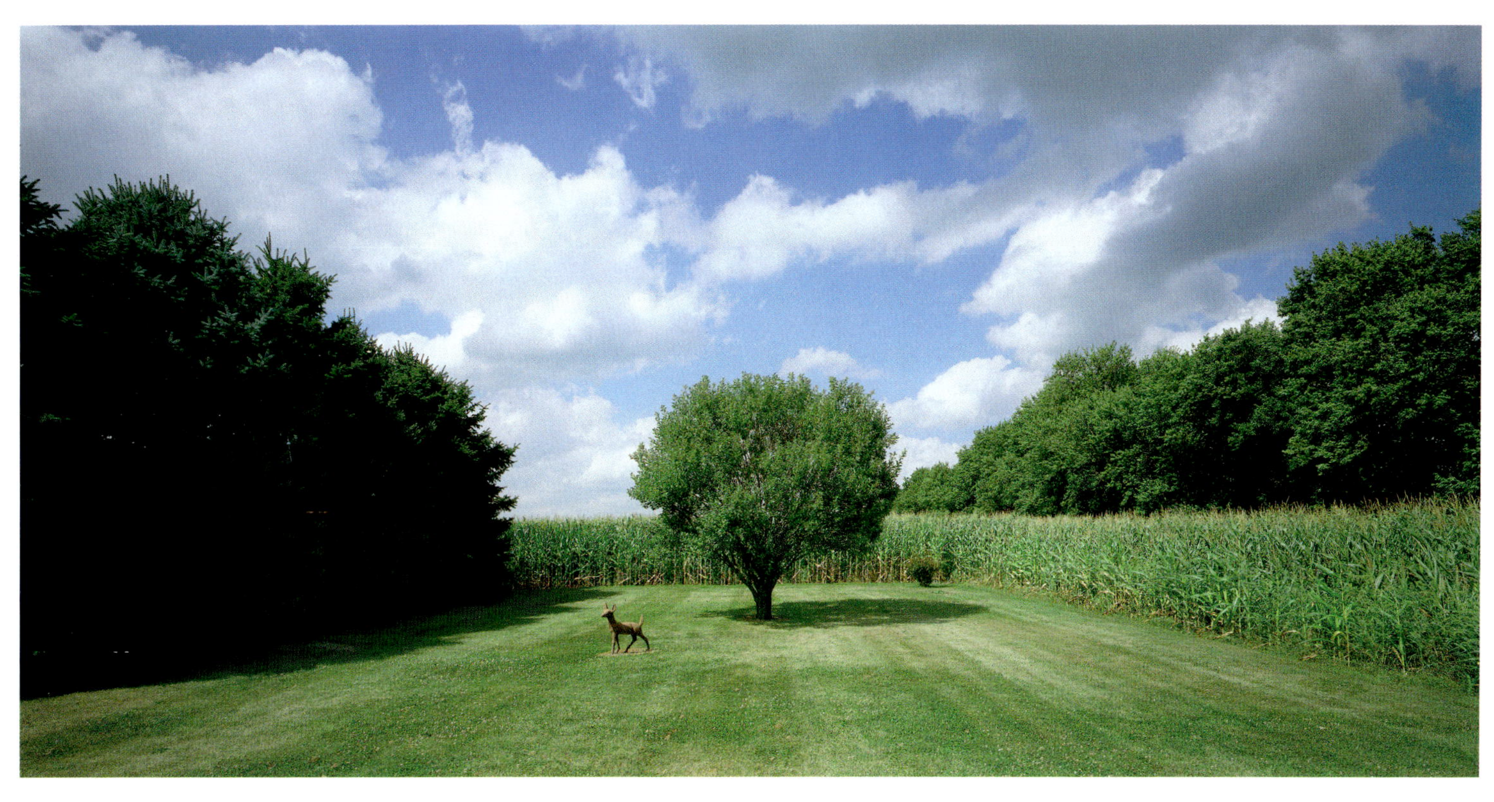

Manhattan, Illinois

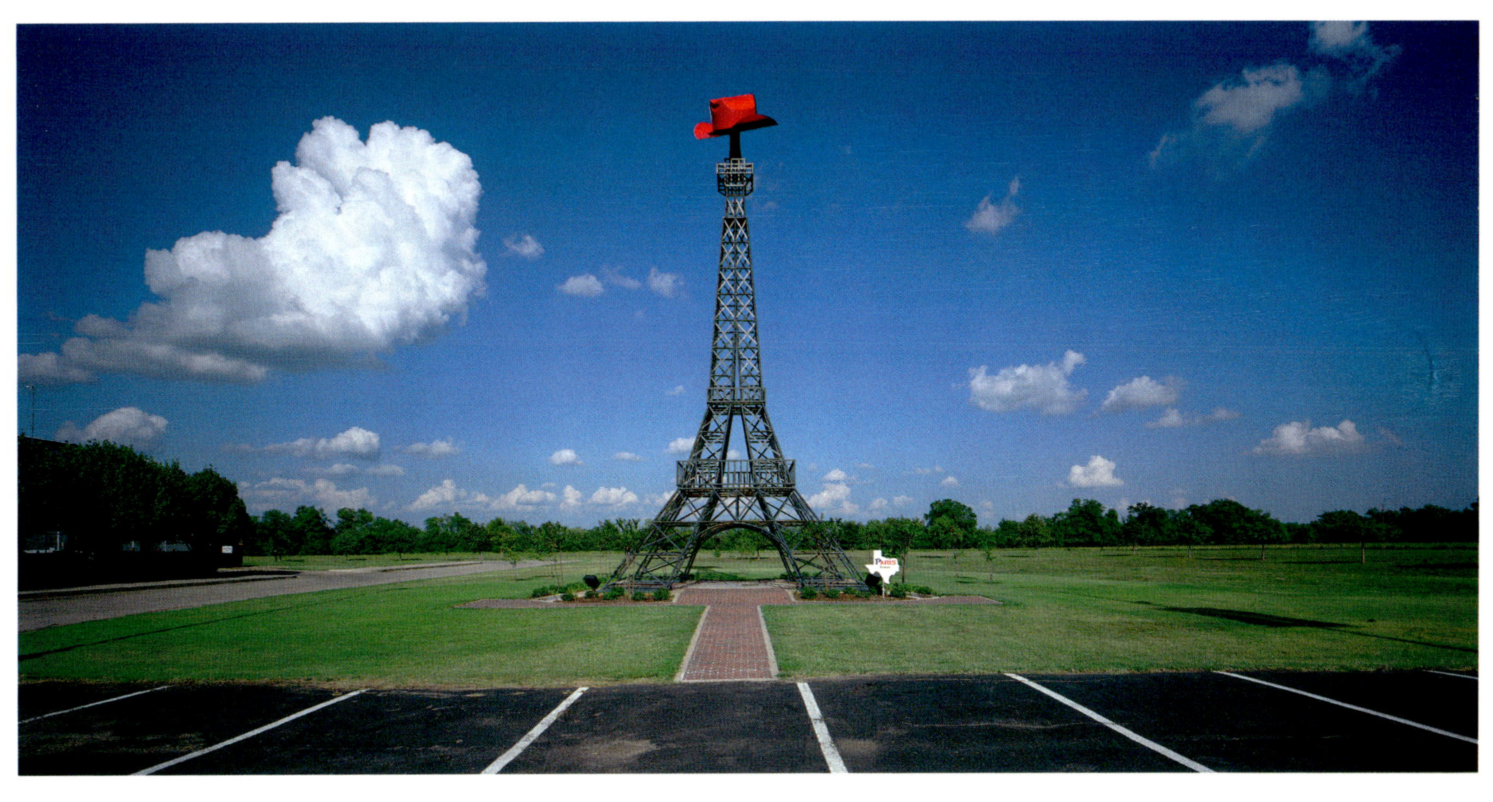

Paris, Texas

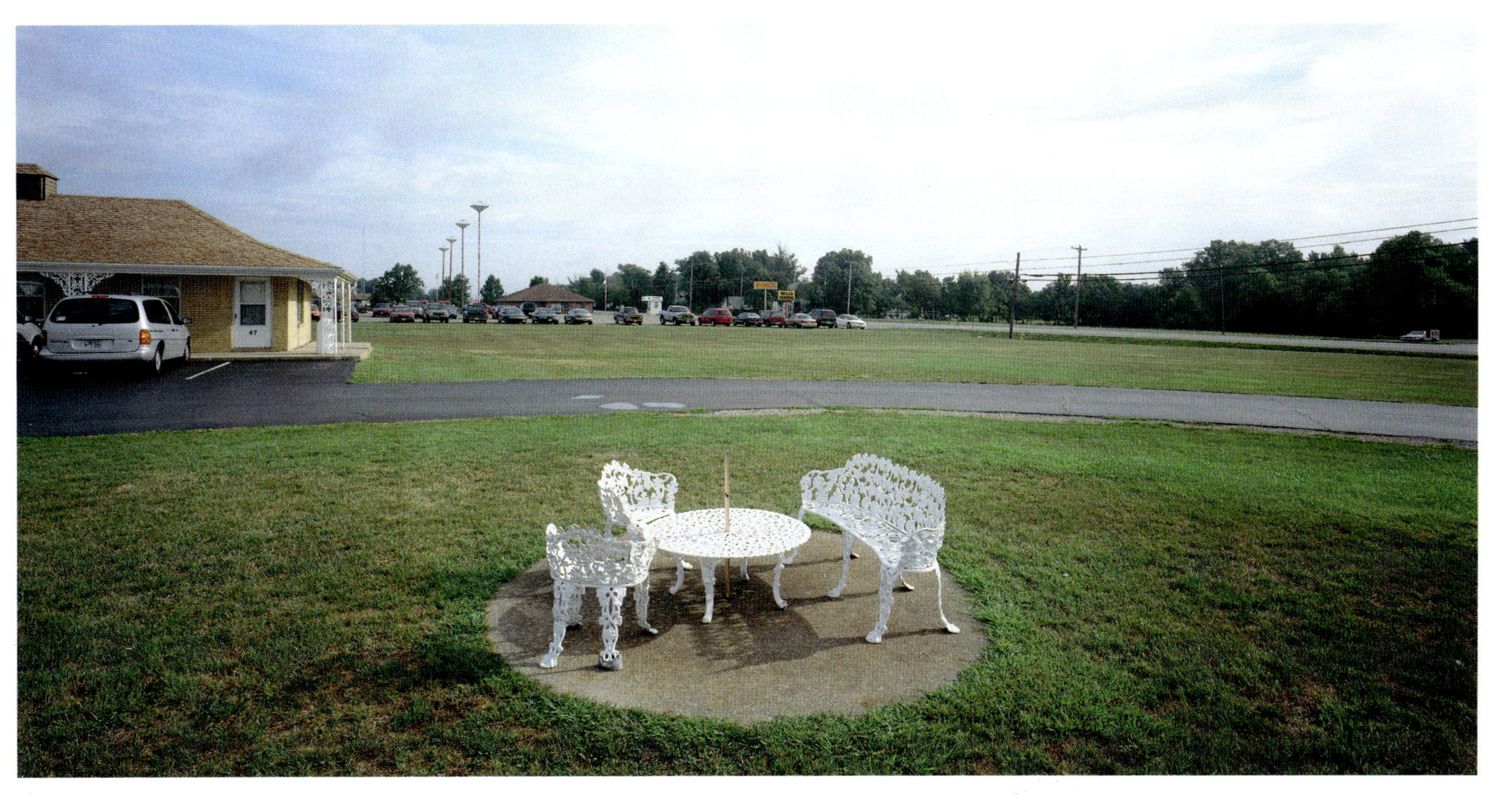

Paris, Illinois

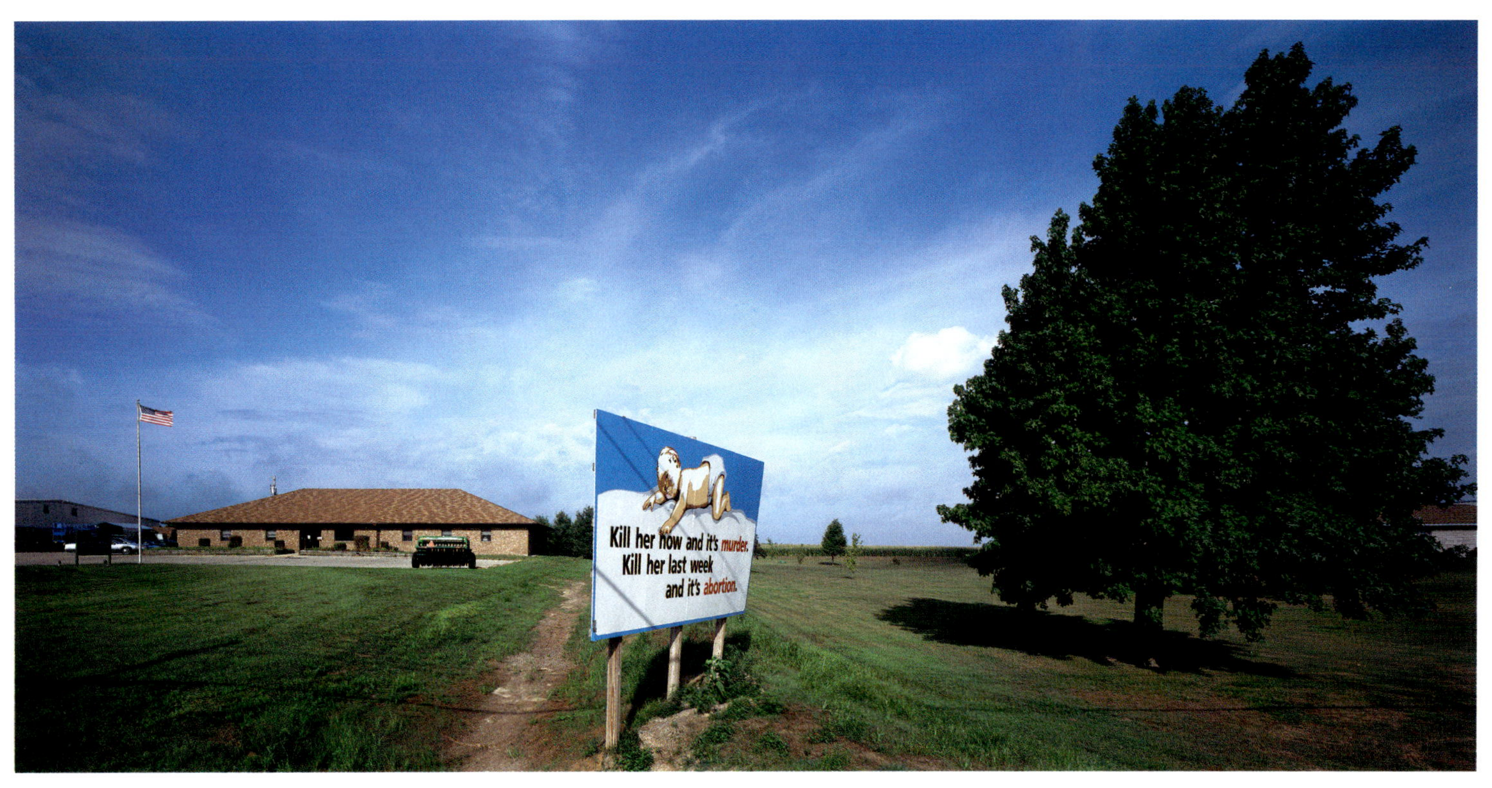

Paris, Illinois

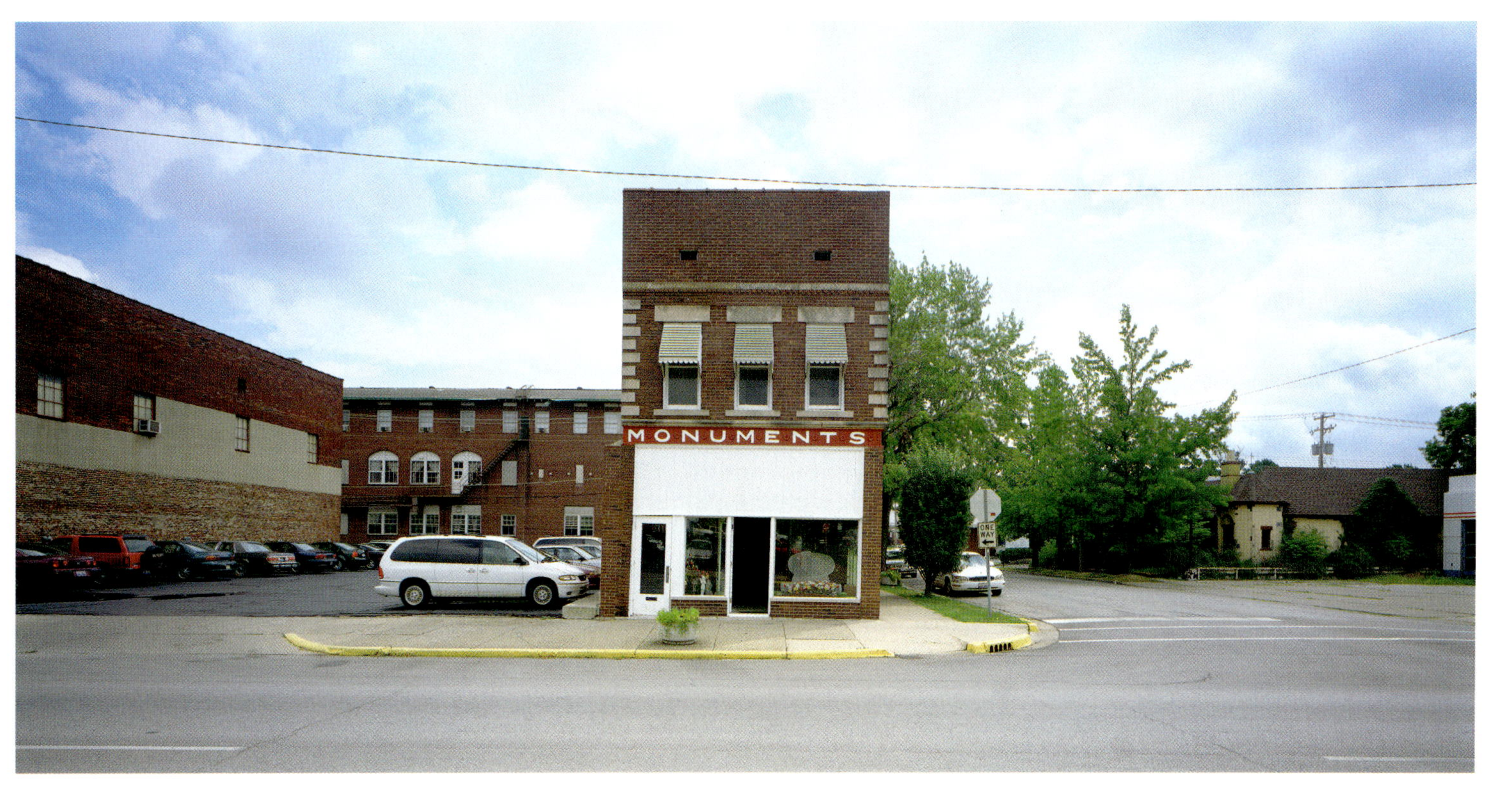

Roma, Illinois

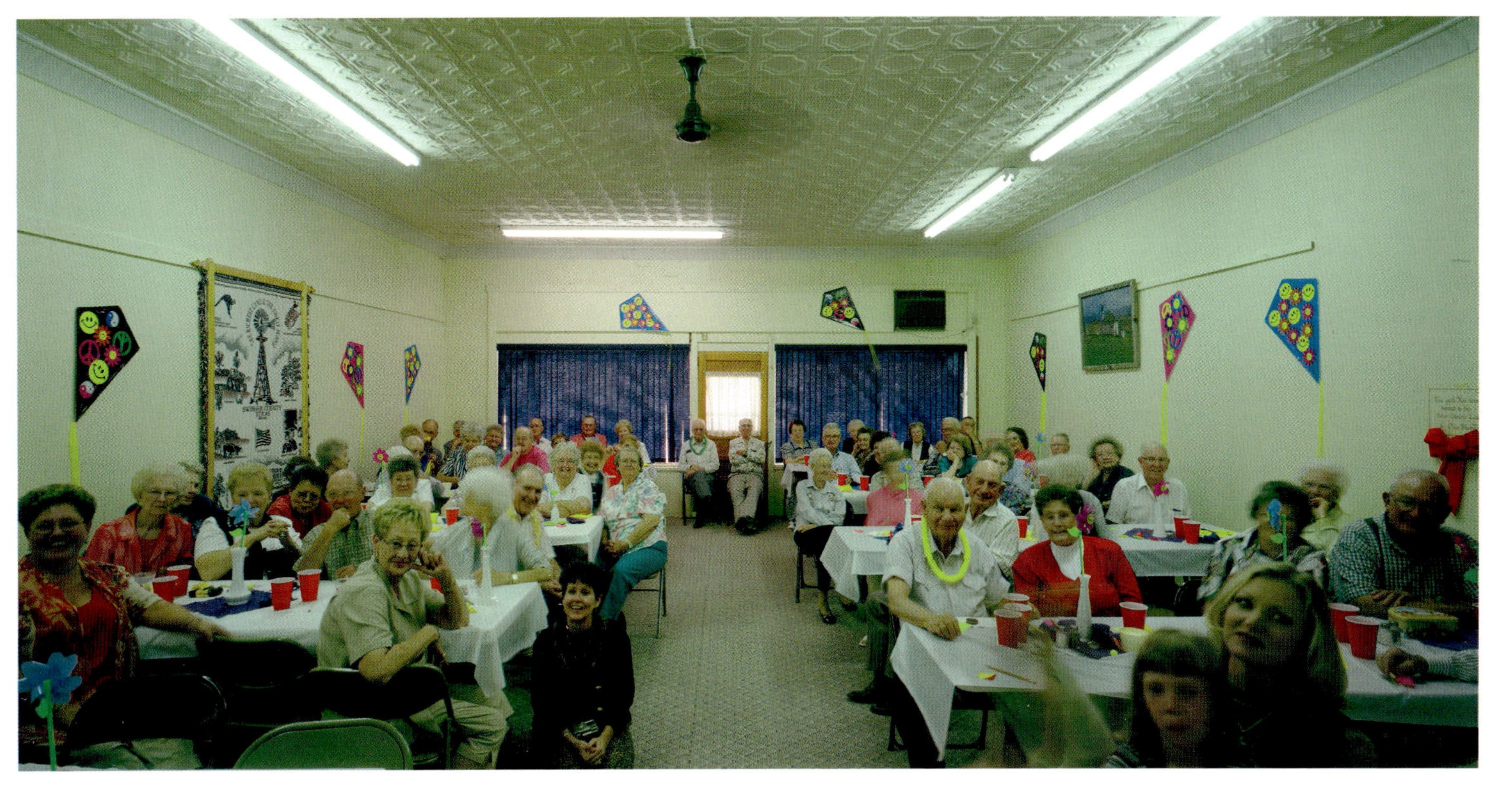

Happy, Texas

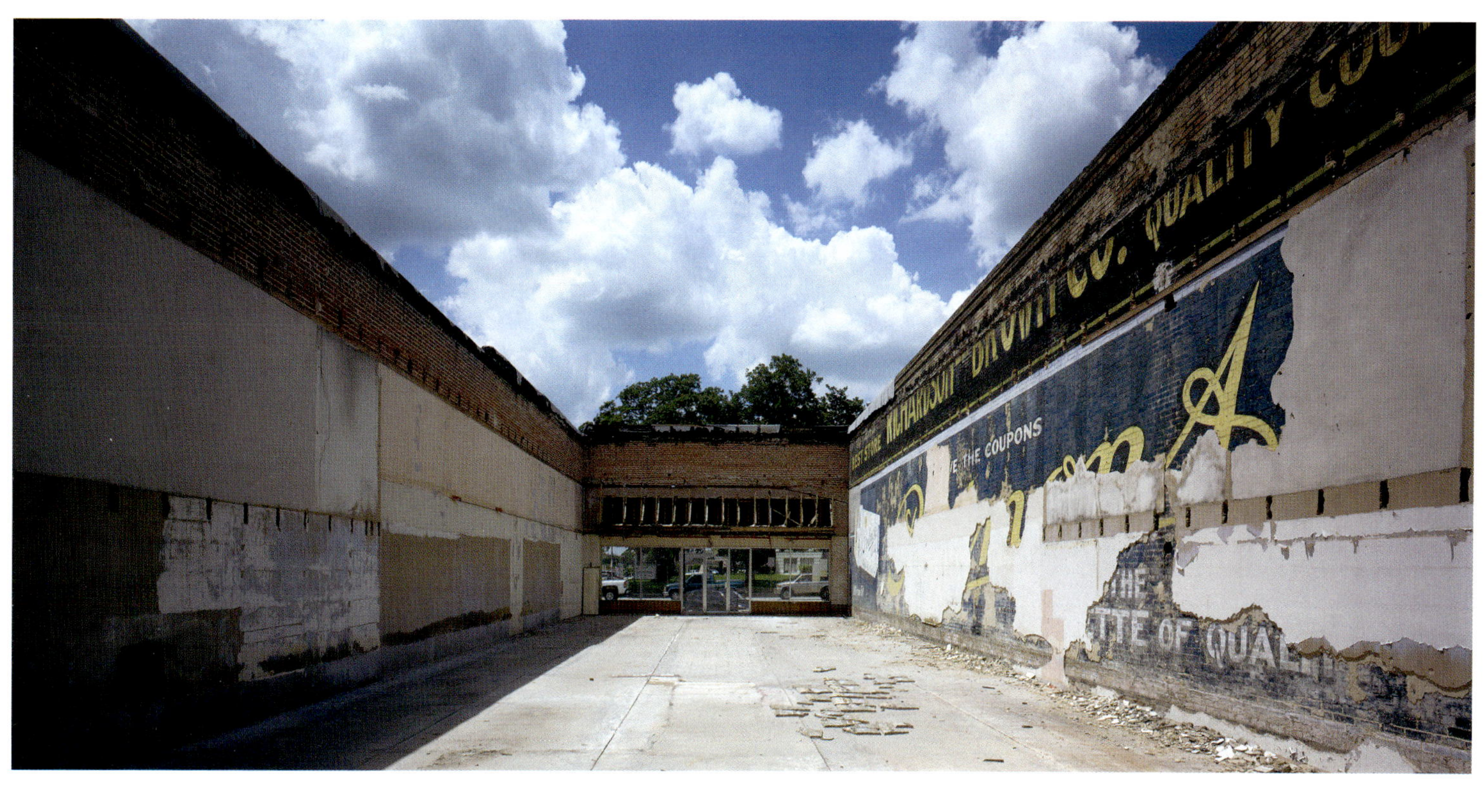

Athens, Texas

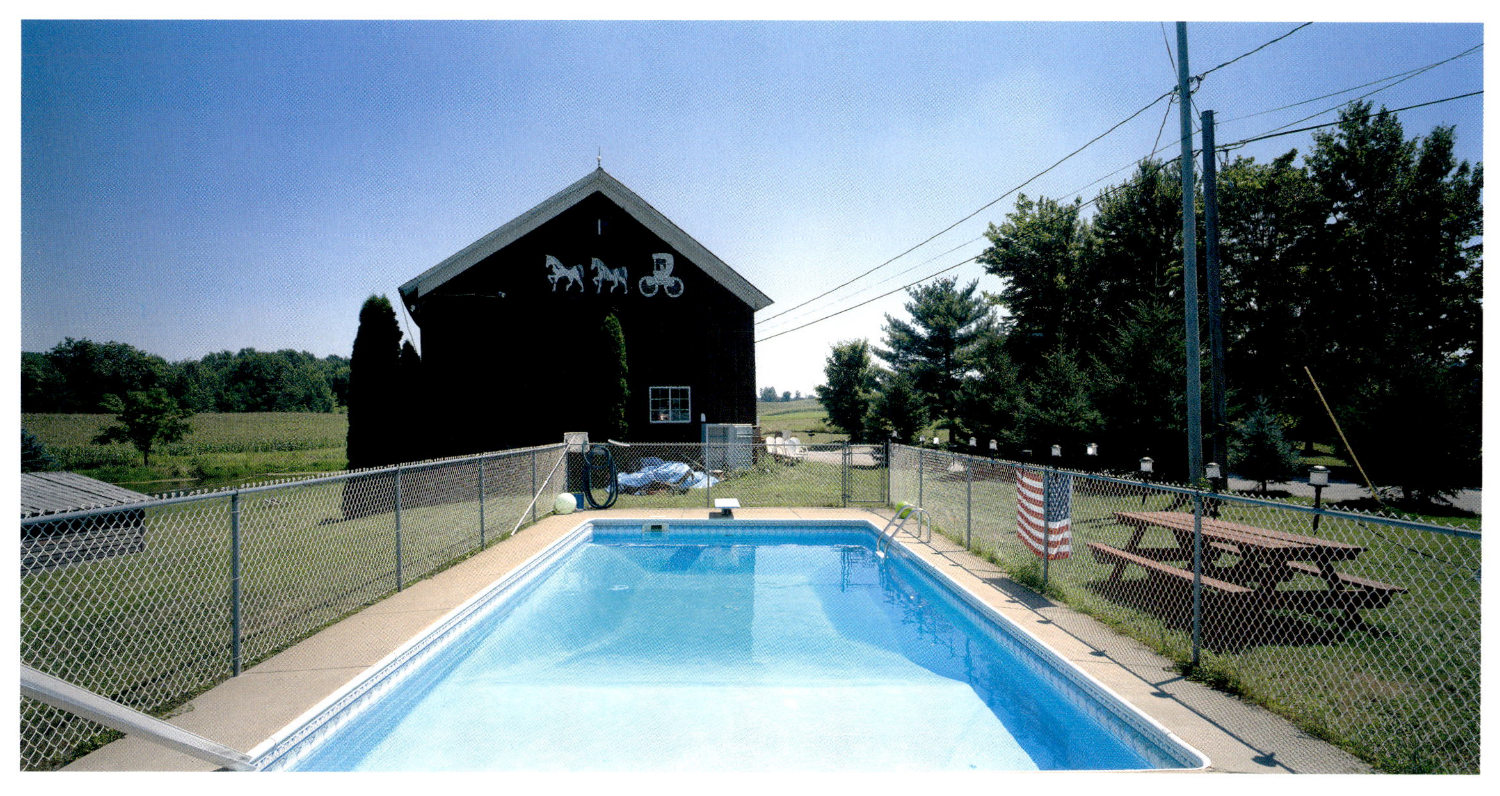

Bagdad, Pennsylvania

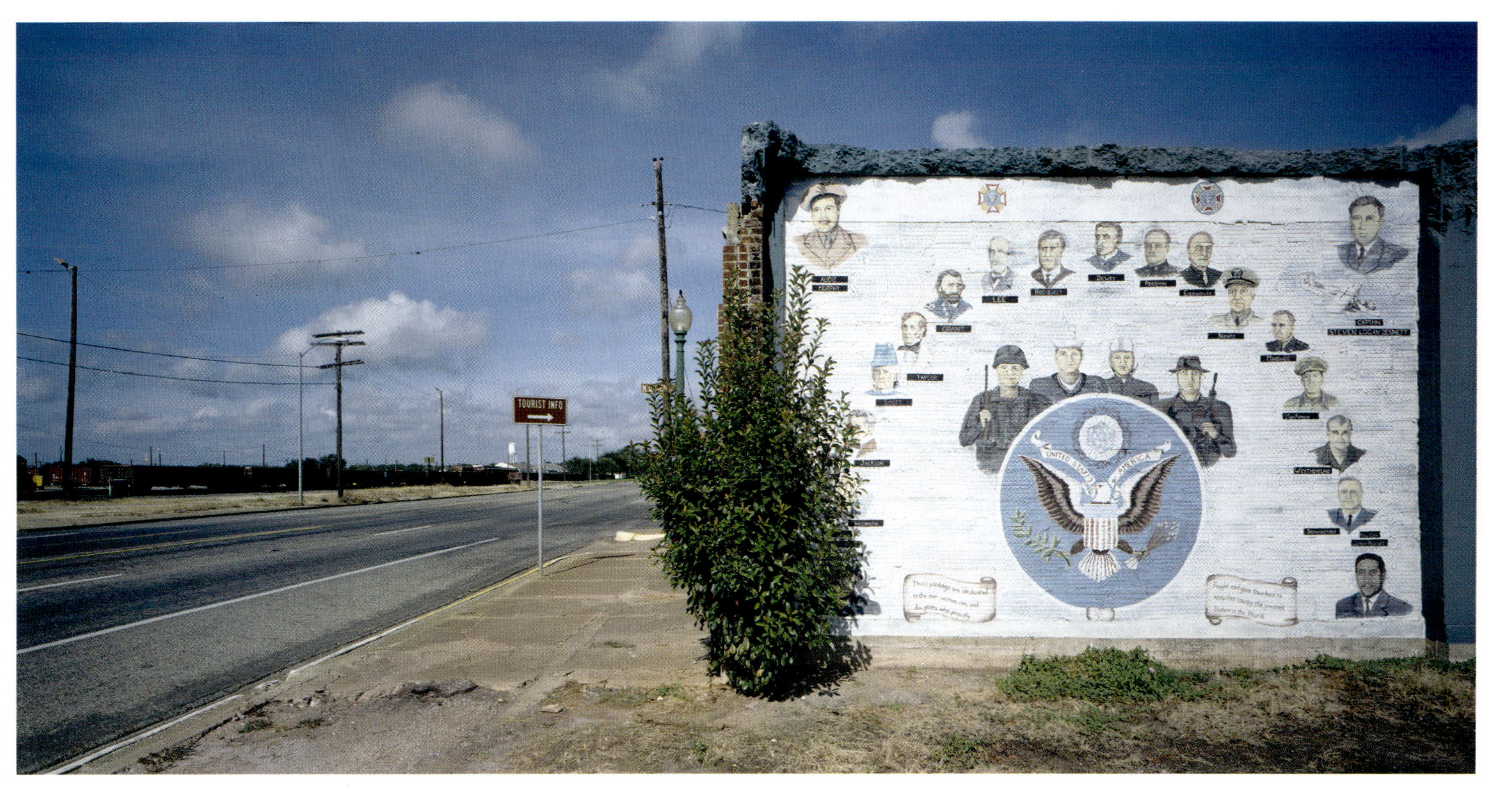

Palestine, Texas

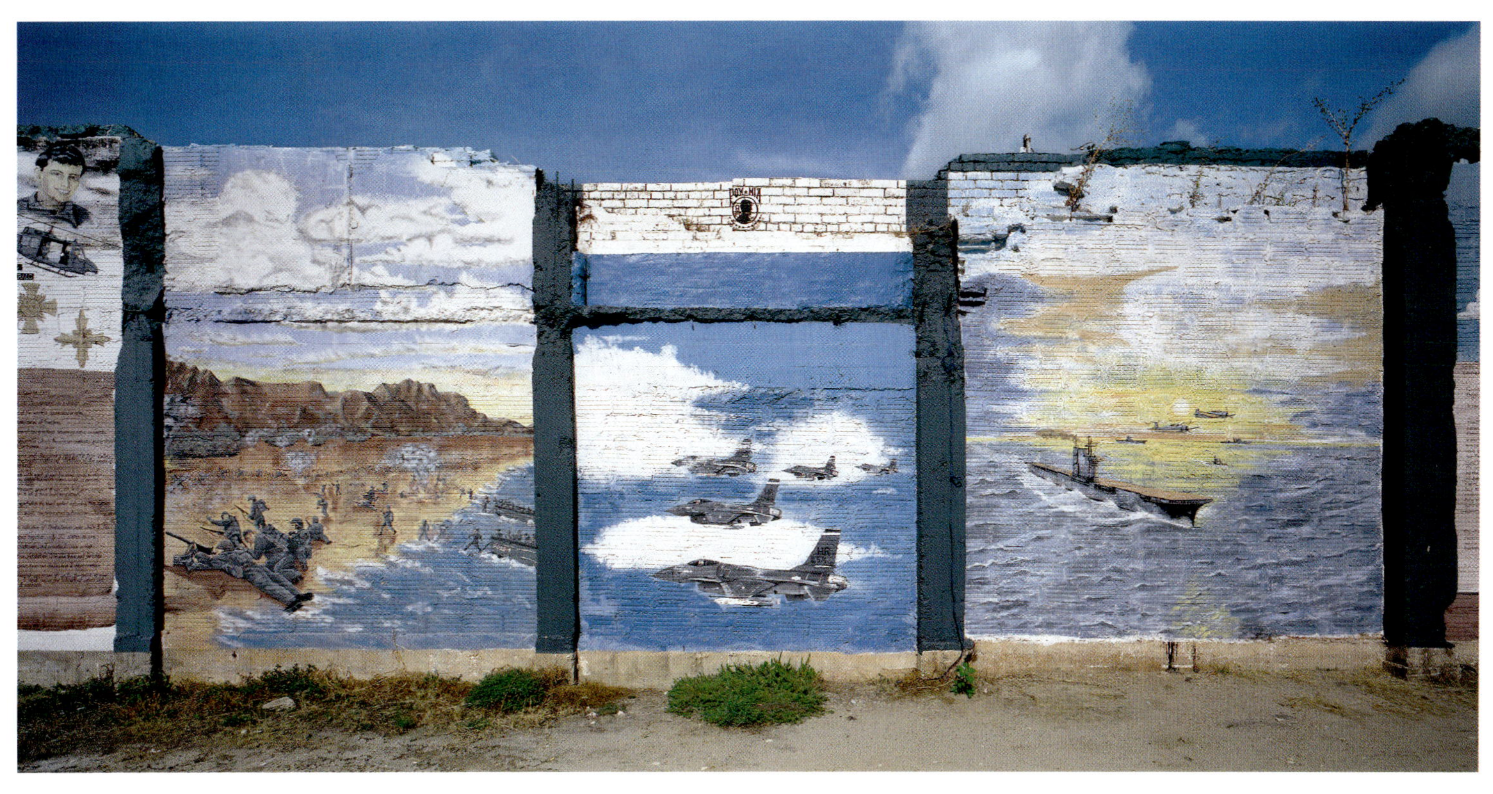

Palestine, Texas

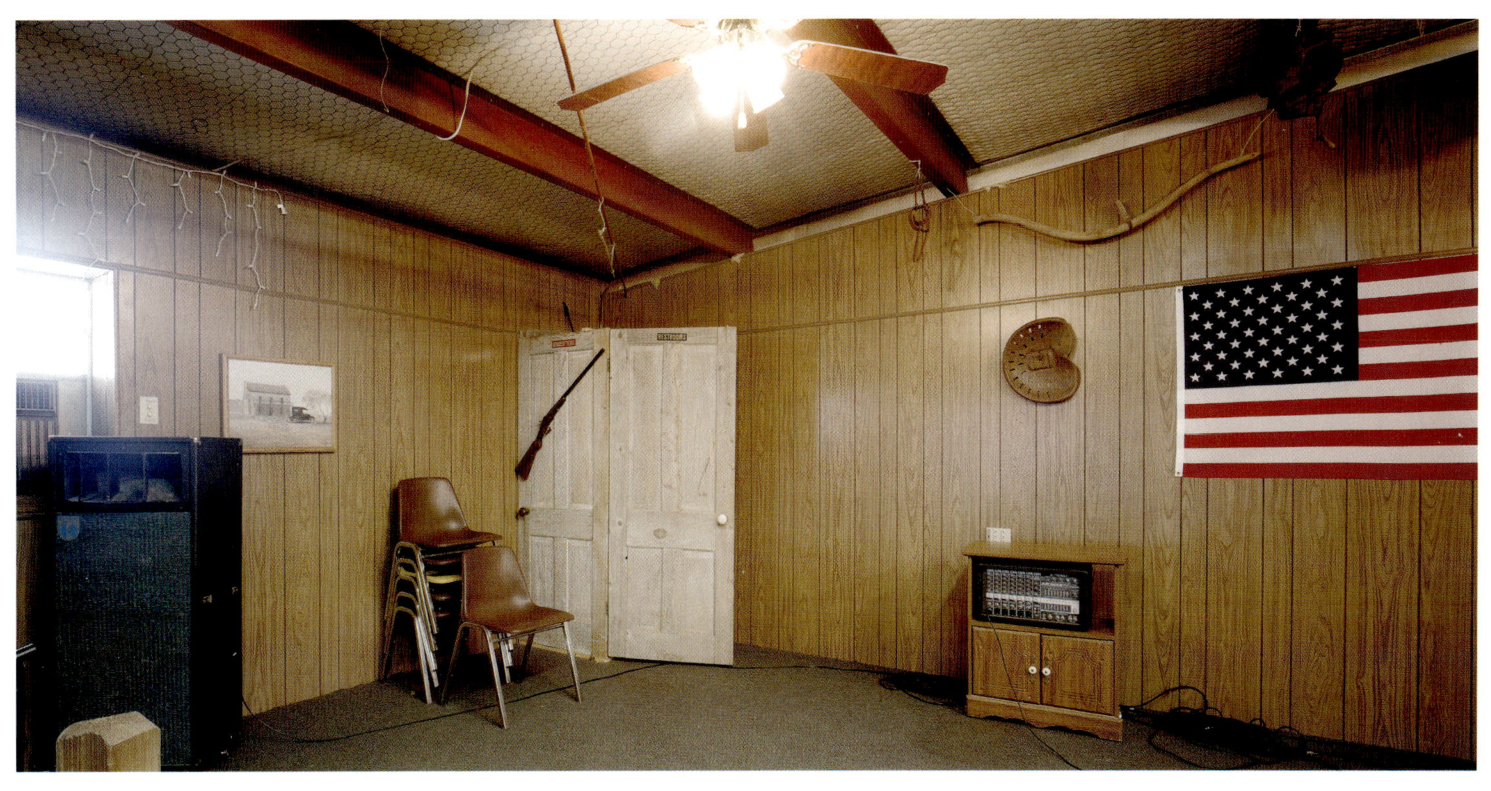

Loving, Texas

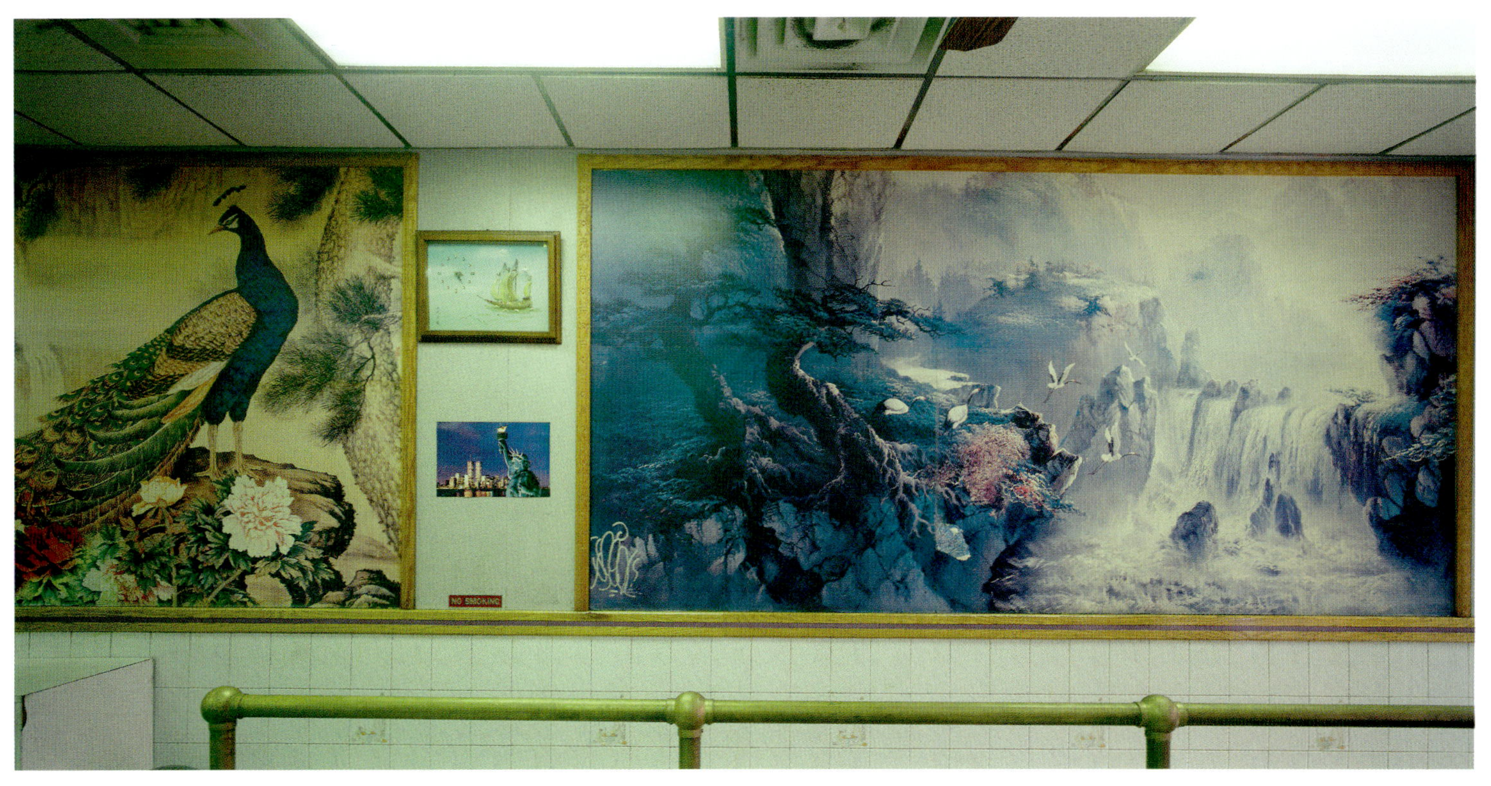

Manhattan, New York

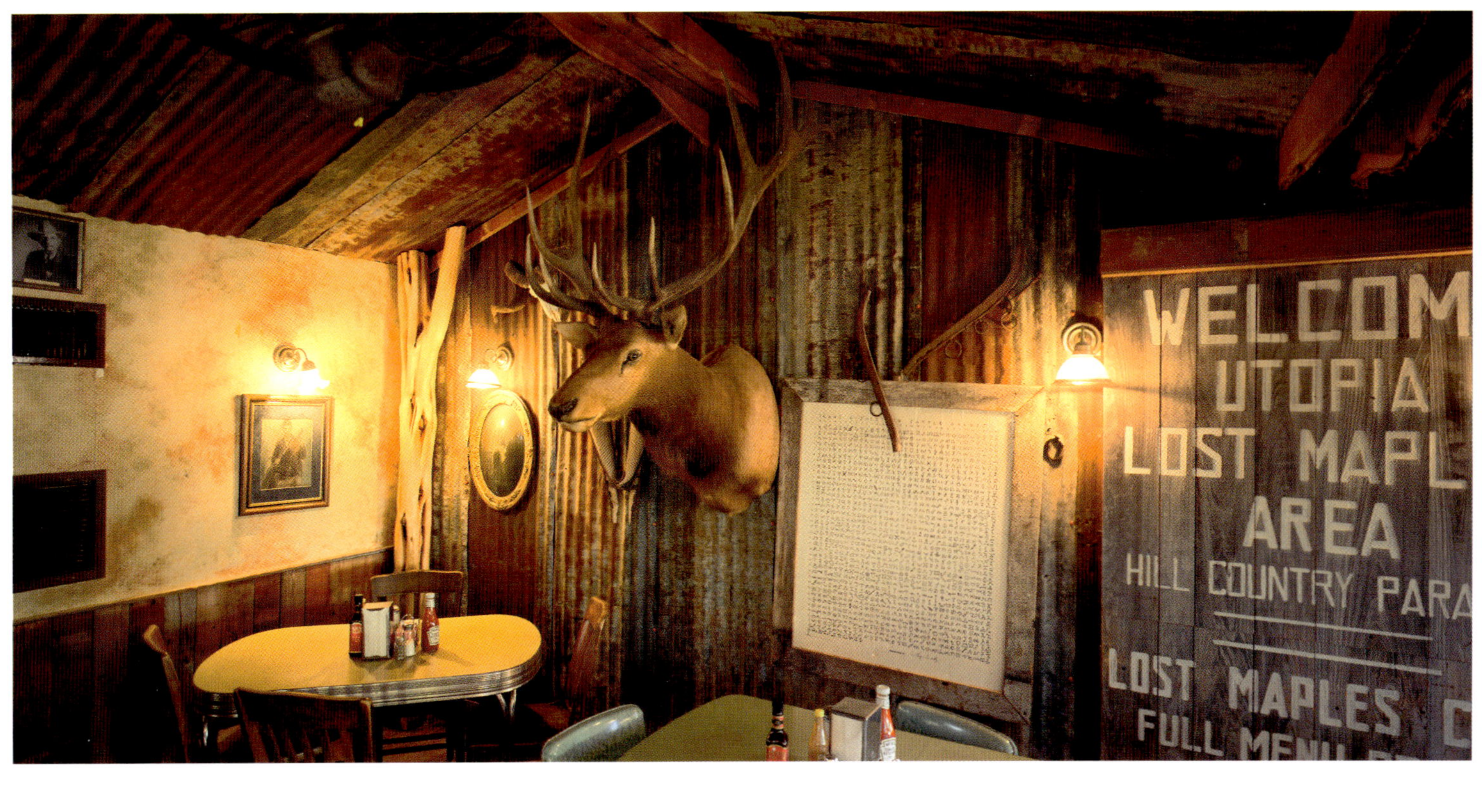

Utopia, Texas

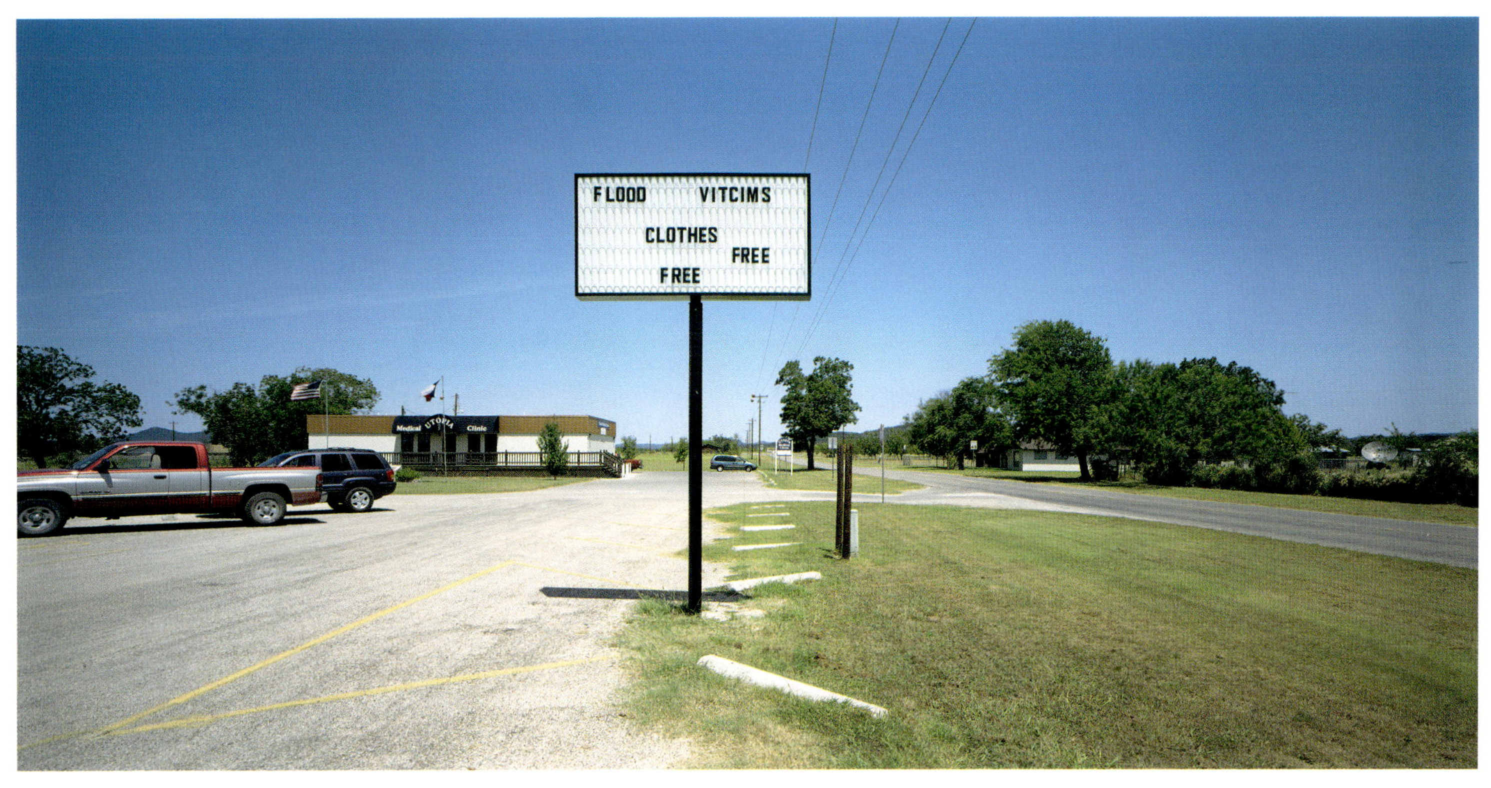

Utopia, Texas

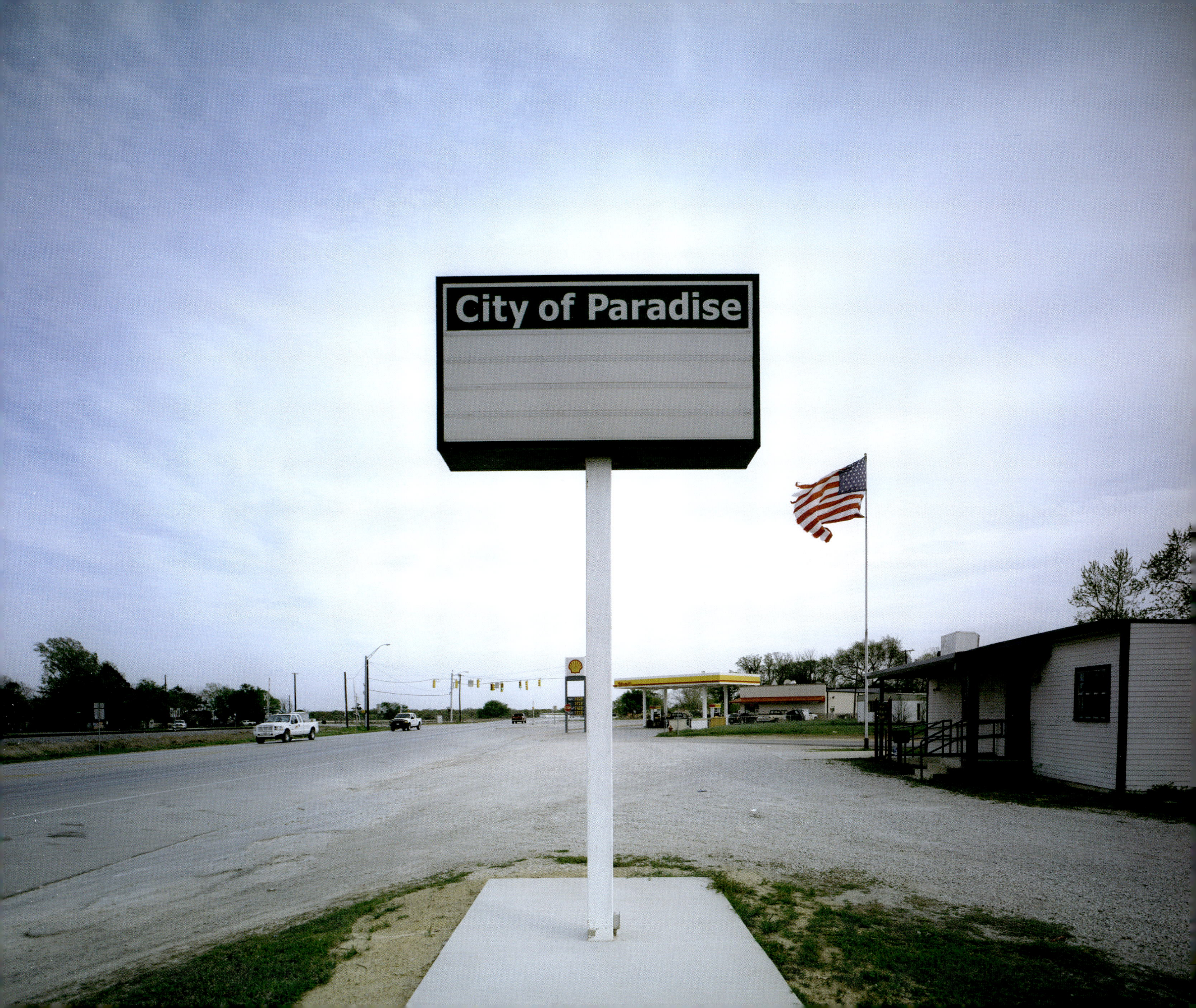
City of Paradise

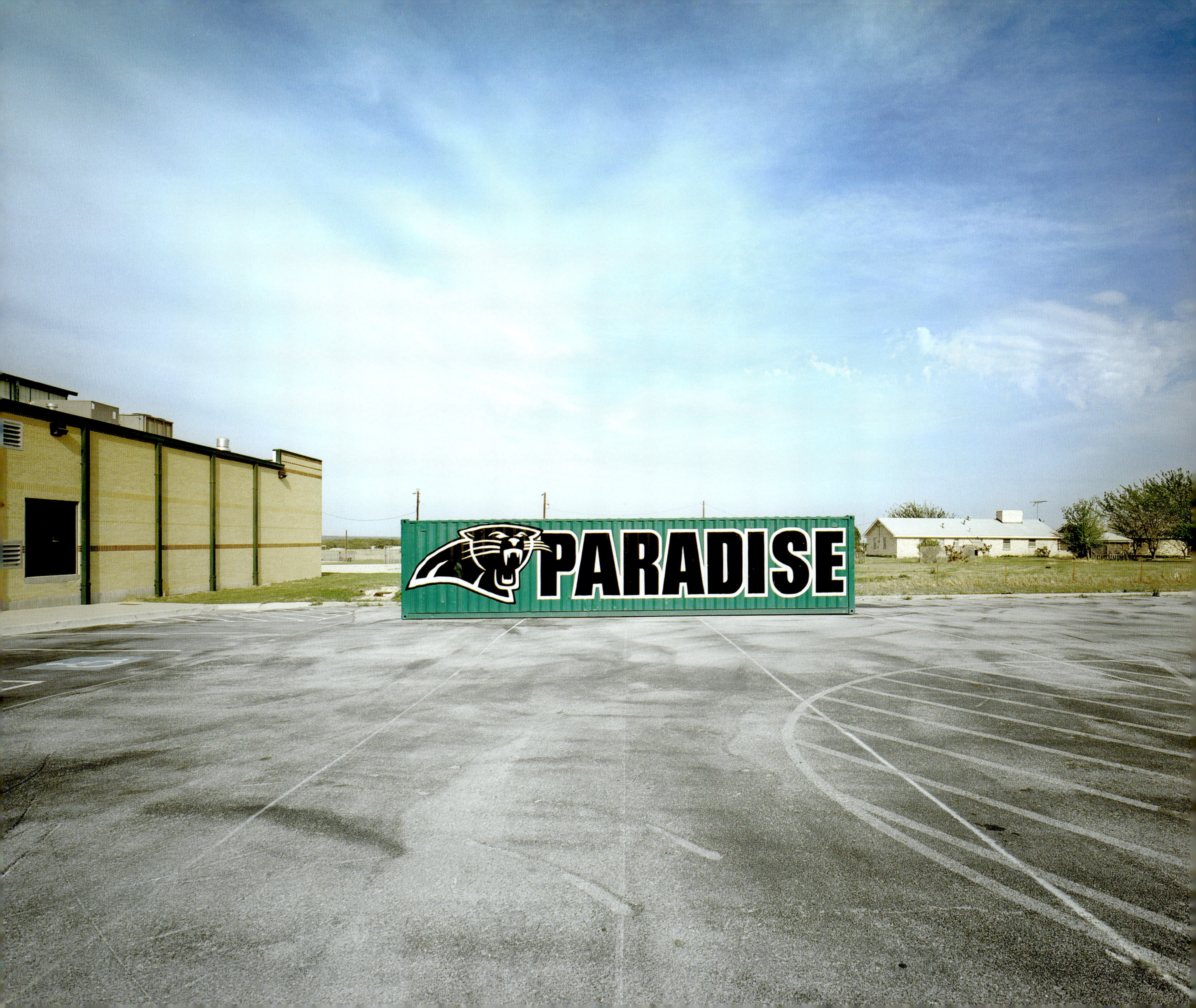
PARADISE

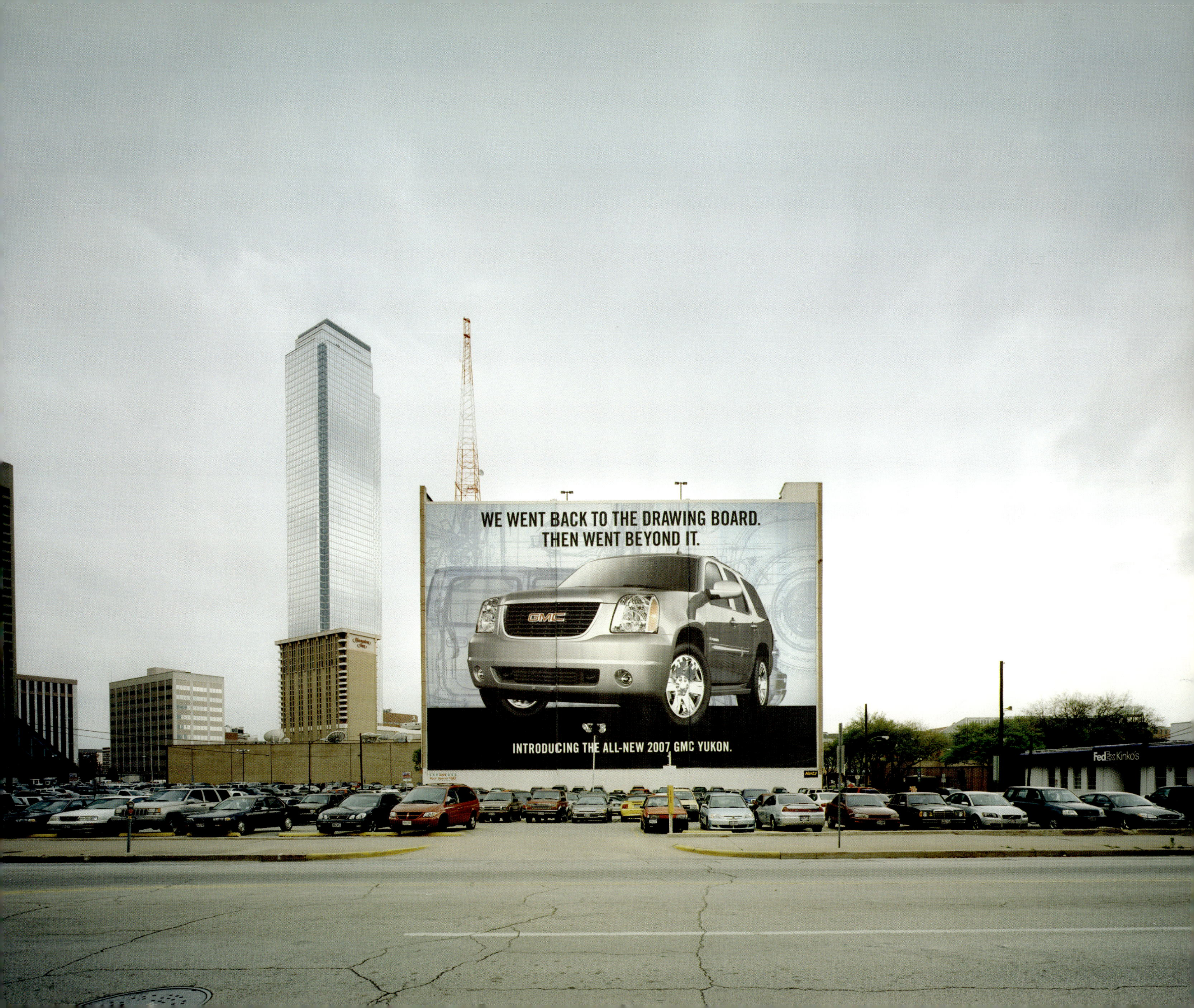

WE WENT BACK TO THE DRAWING BOARD.
THEN WENT BEYOND IT.
GMC
INTRODUCING THE ALL-NEW 2007 GMC YUKON.
FedEx Kinko's

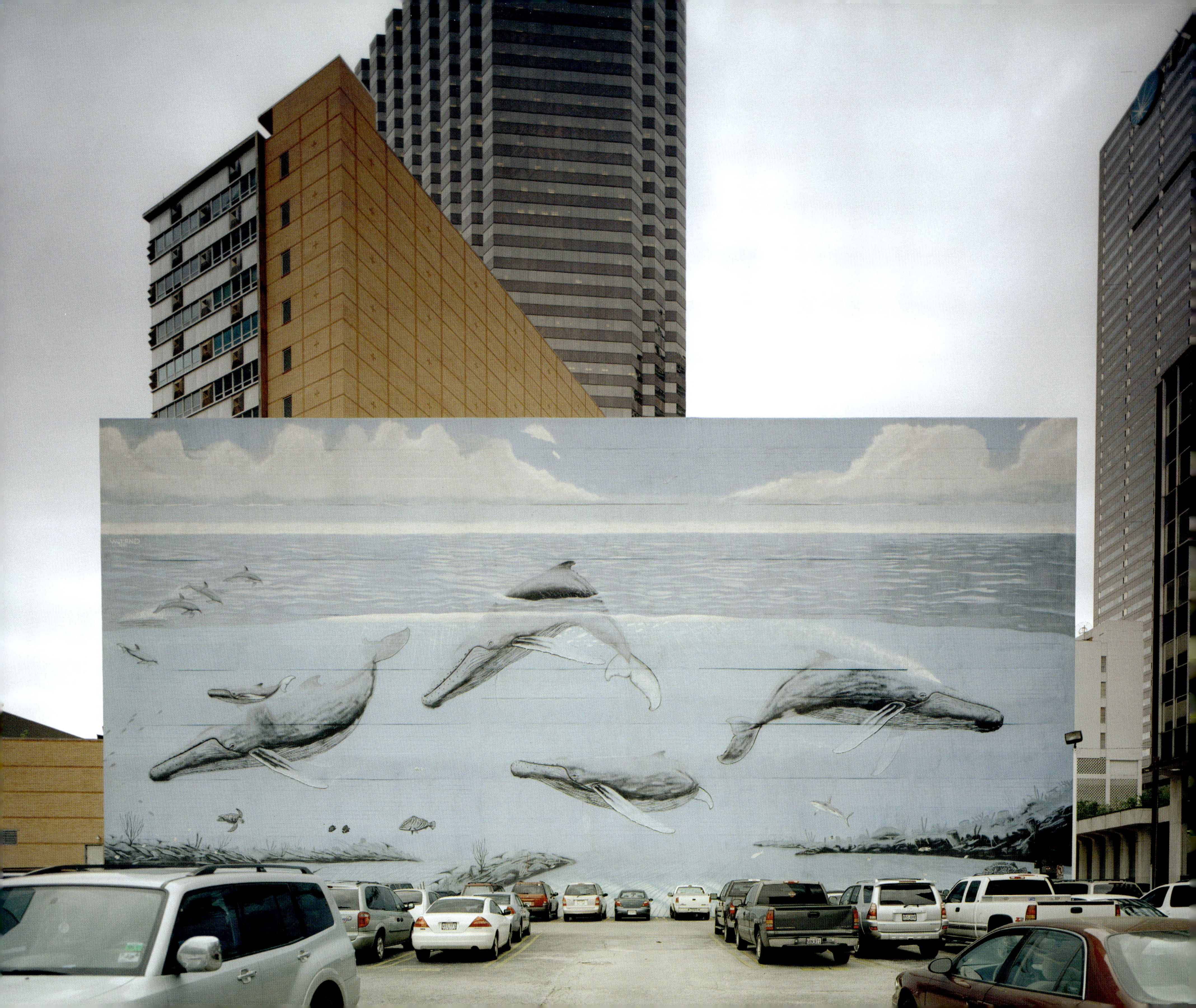

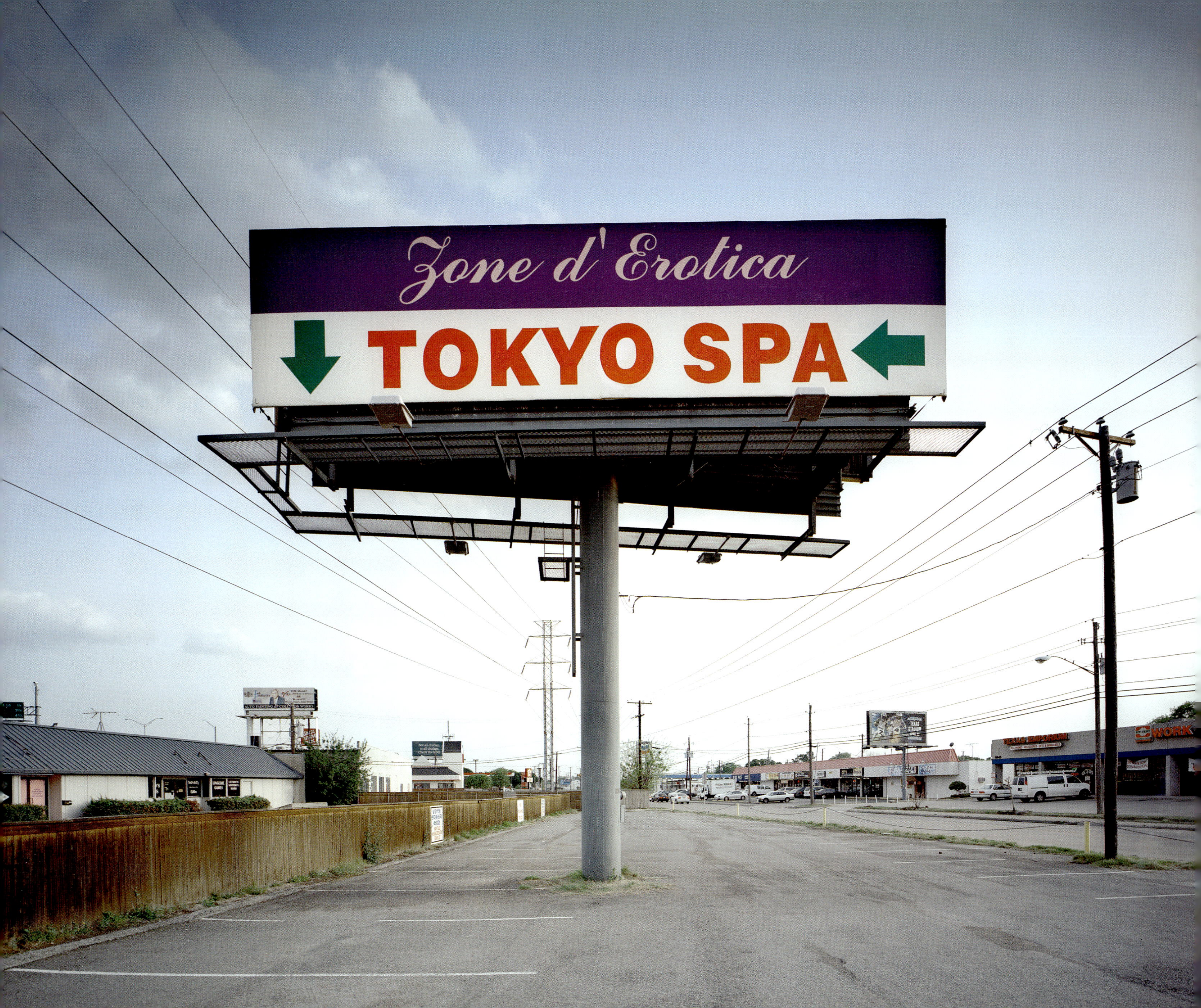
Zone d'Erotica
TOKYO SPA

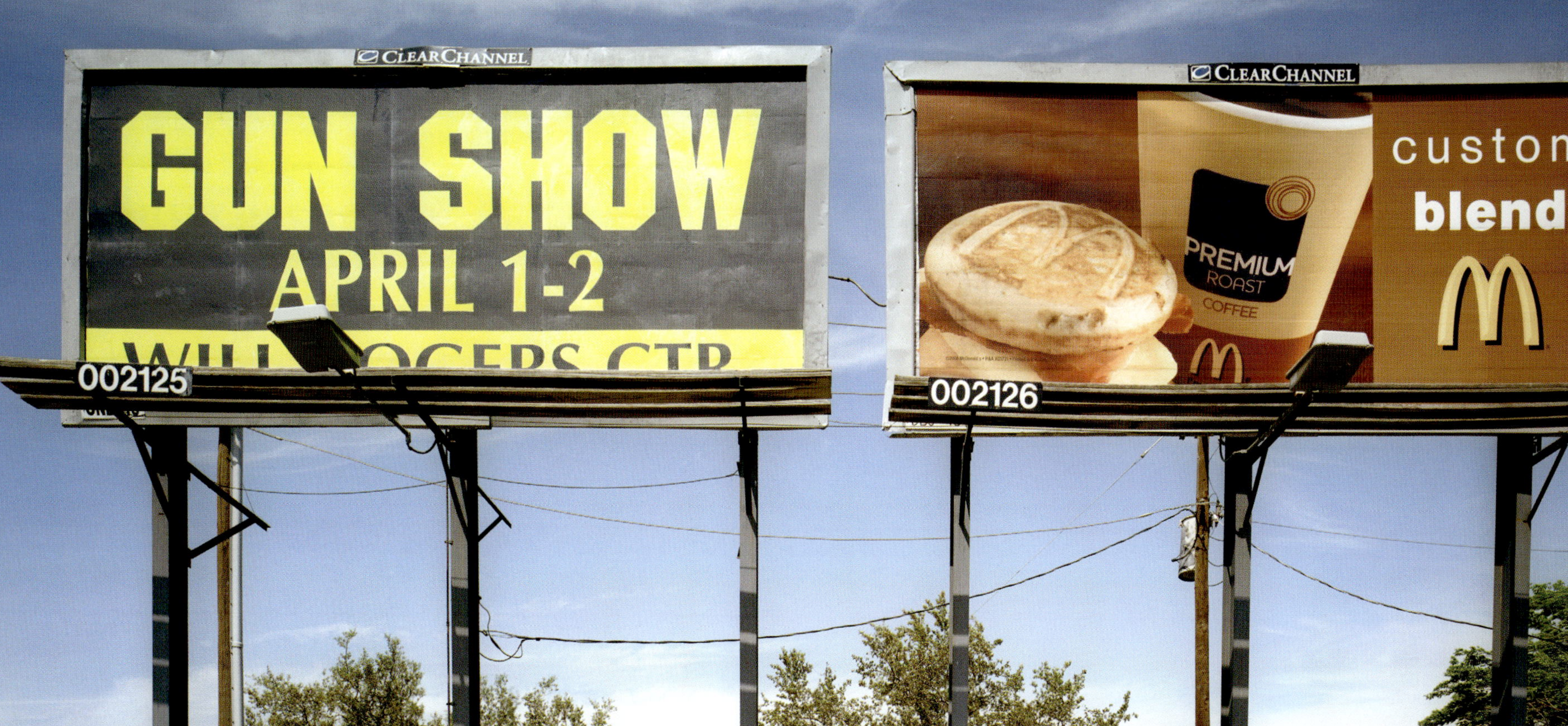
CLEAR CHANNEL
GUN SHOW
APRIL 1-2
ROGERS CTR.
002125
CLEAR CHANNEL
custom
blend
PREMIUM
ROAST
COFFEE
002126

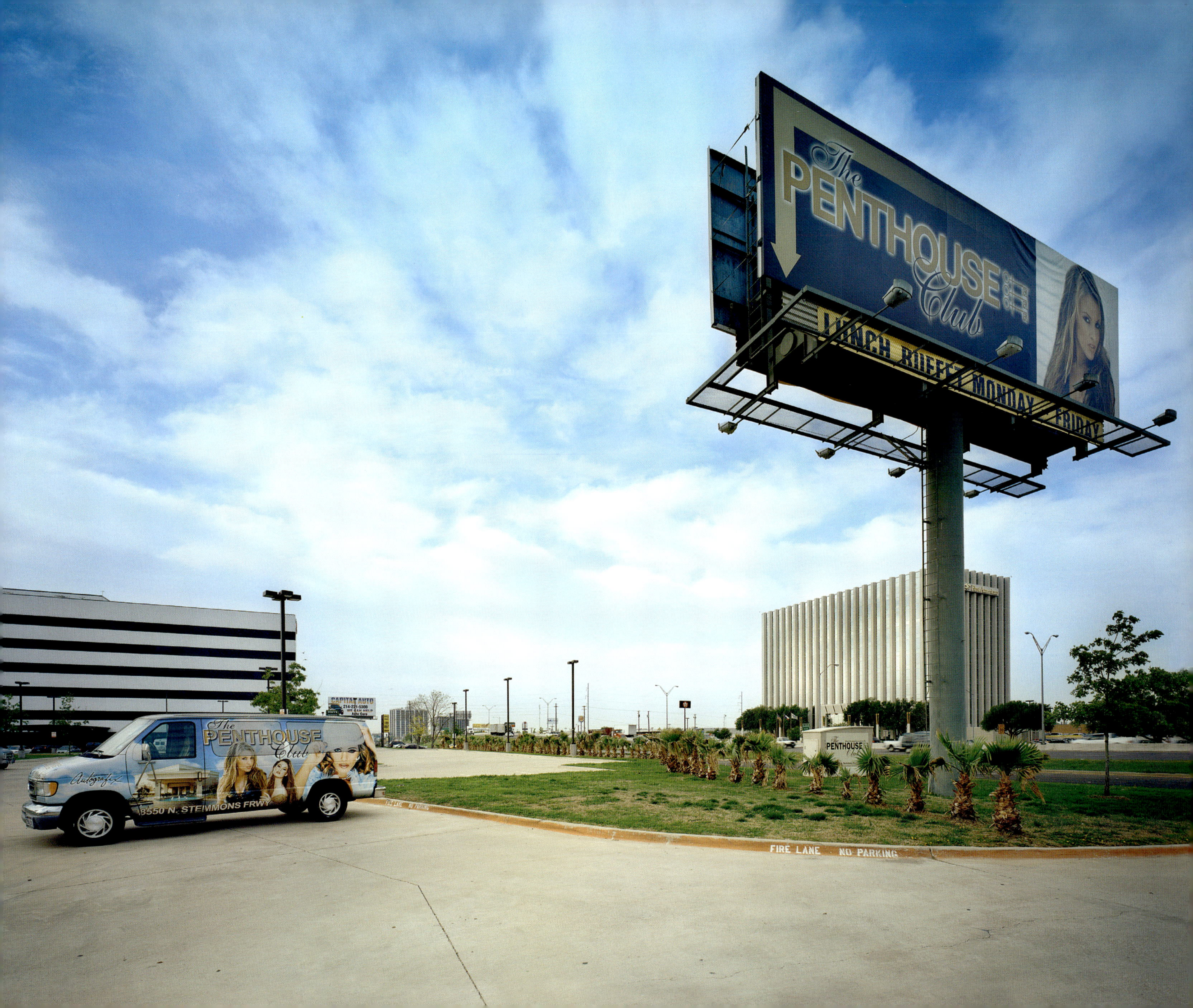
The
PENTHOUSE
Club
LUNCH BUFFET MONDAY FRIDAY
The
PENTHOUSE
Club
Autografix
8550 N. STEMMONS FRWY
CAPITAL AUTO
214-221-5000
THE PENTHOUSE
FIRE LANE NO PARKING

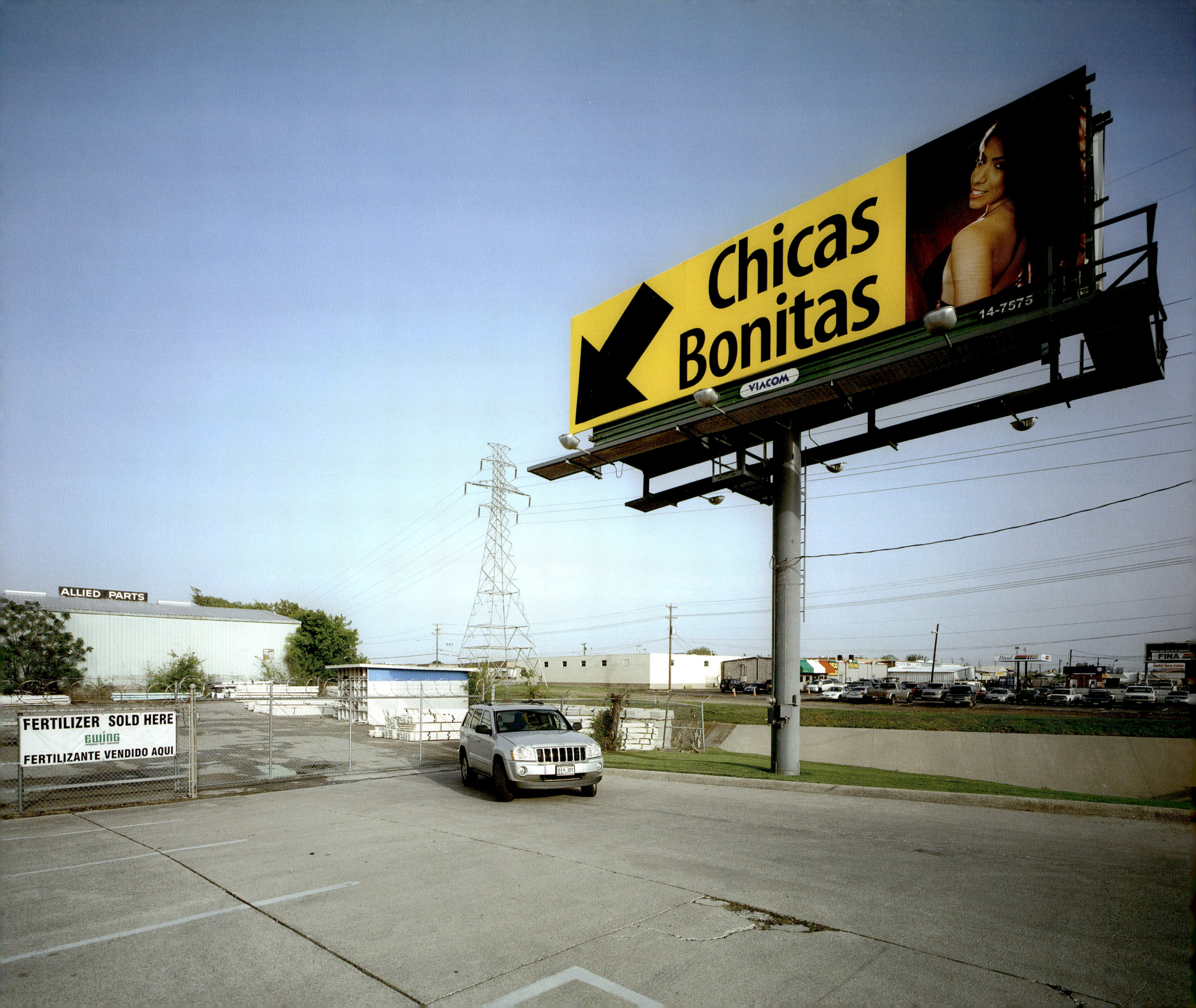

Chicas
Bonitas
14-7575
VIACOM
ALLIED PARTS
FERTILIZER SOLD HERE
EWING
FERTILIZANTE VENDIDO AQUI
FINA
Diesel

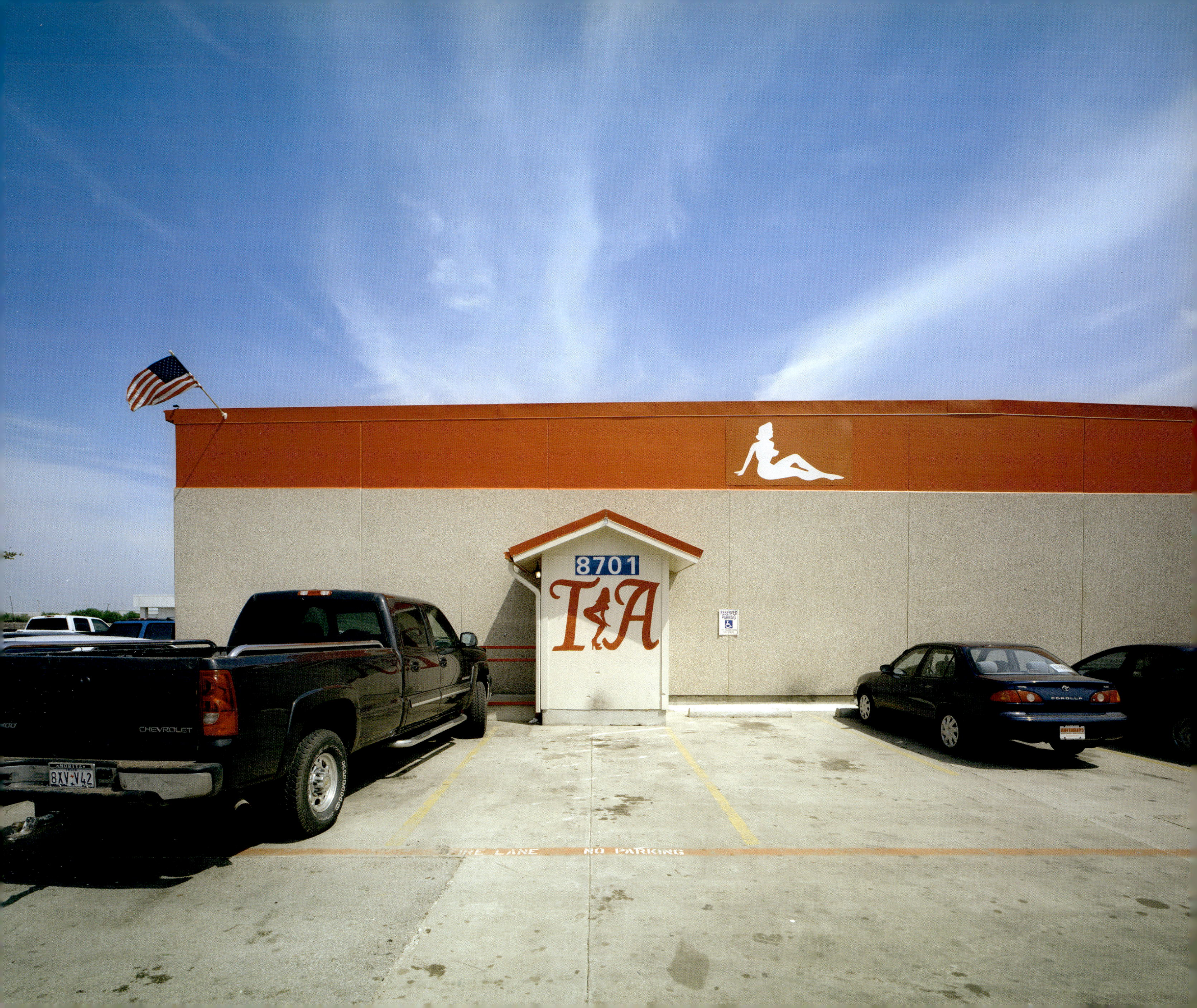

8701
T A
RESERVED PARKING
CHEVROLET
8XV-V42
FIRE LANE   NO PARKING
COROLLA

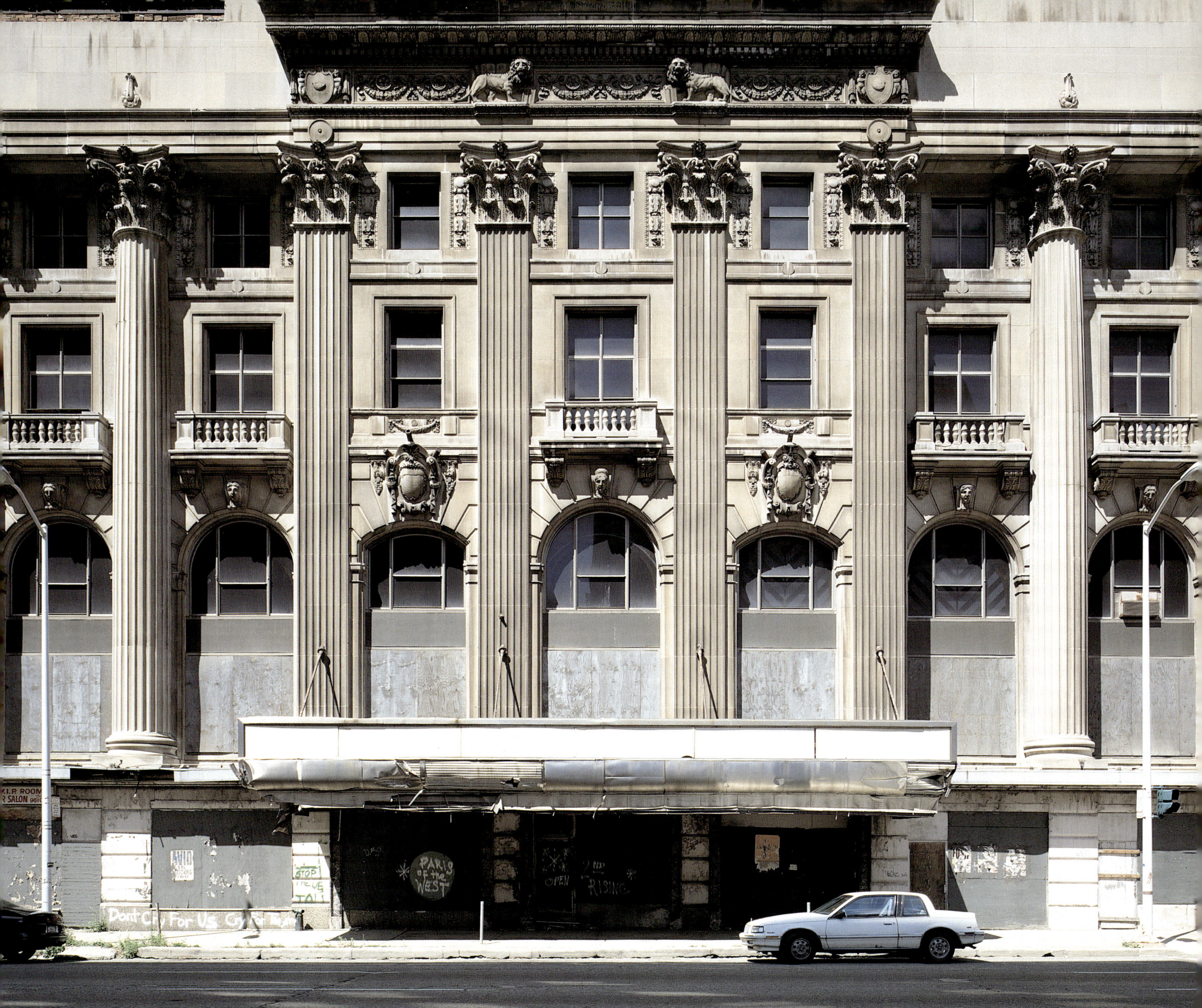

V.I.P. ROOM
R SALON 9610
PARIS OF THE WEST
OPEN
2ND RISING
Don't Cry For Us
AVID

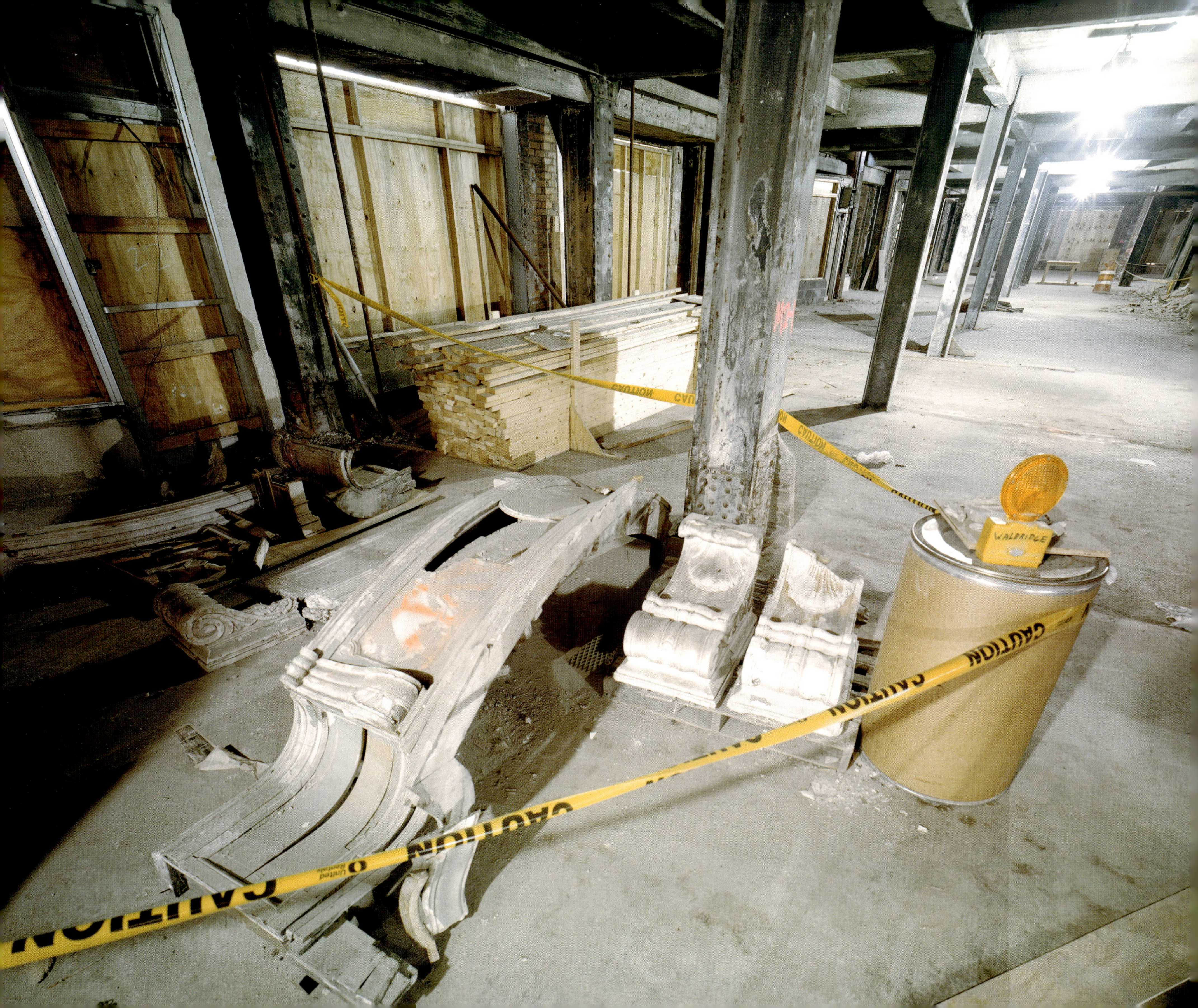

CAUTION
WALBRIDGE
United States

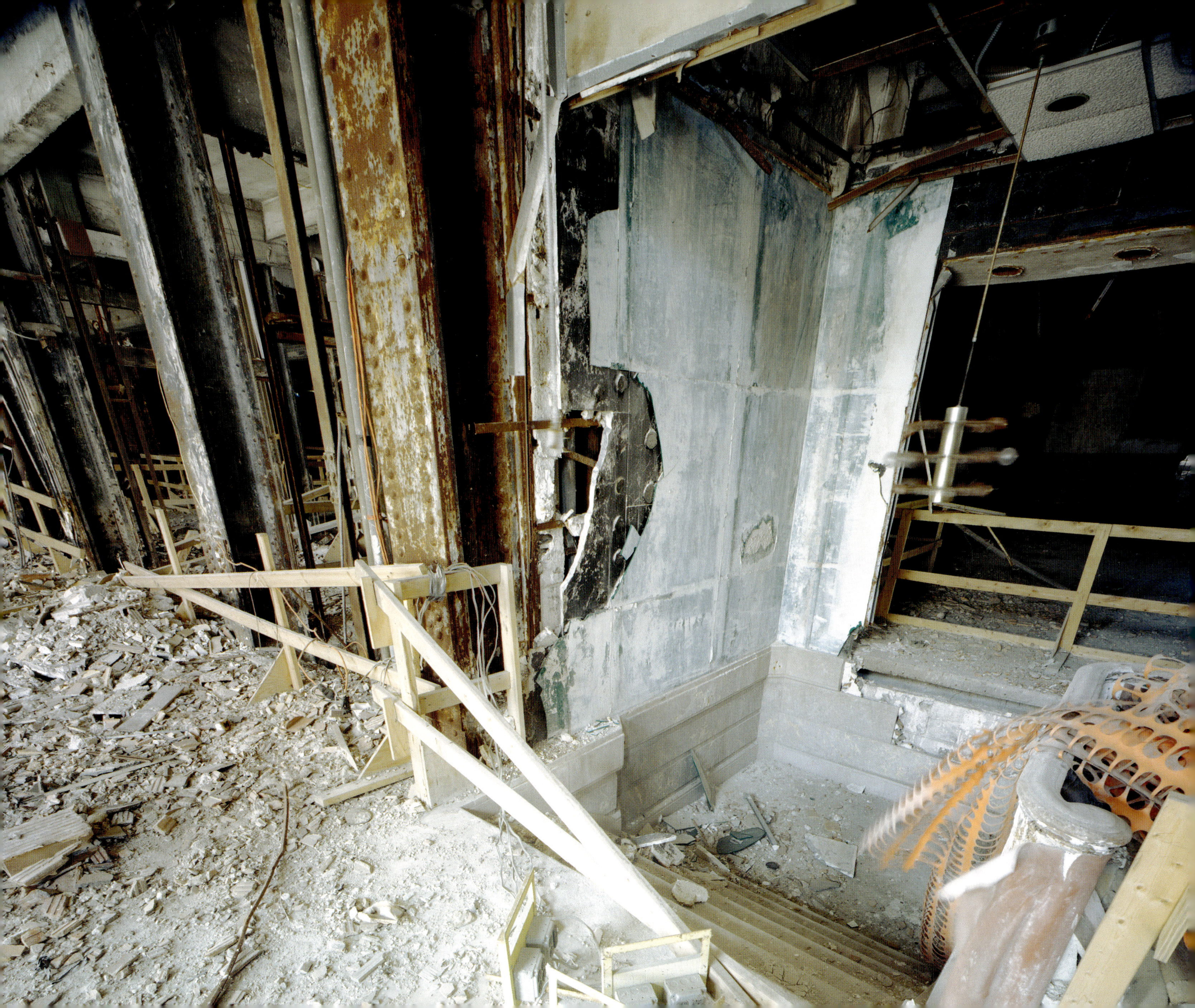

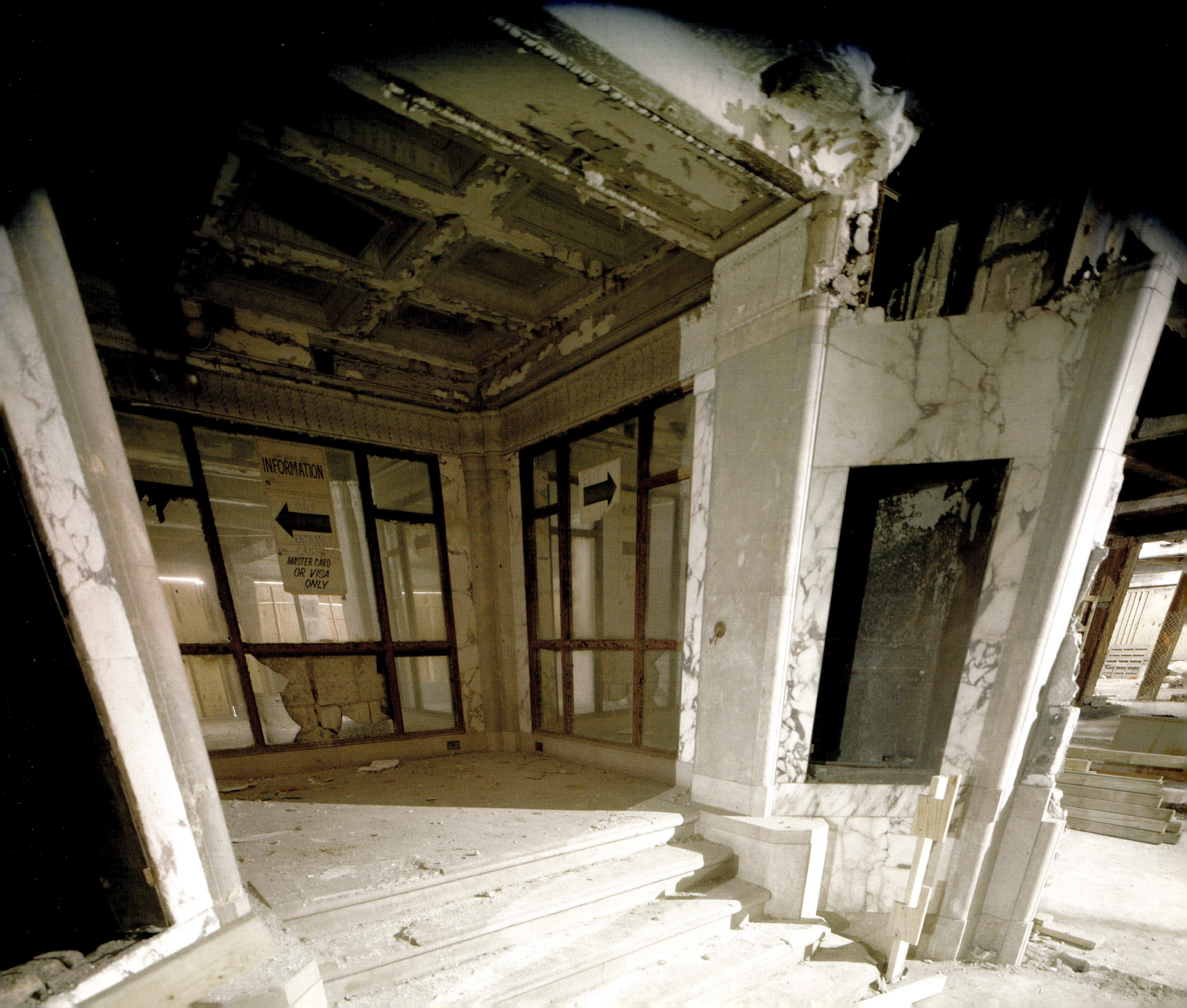
INFORMATION
MASTER CARD
OR VISA
ONLY

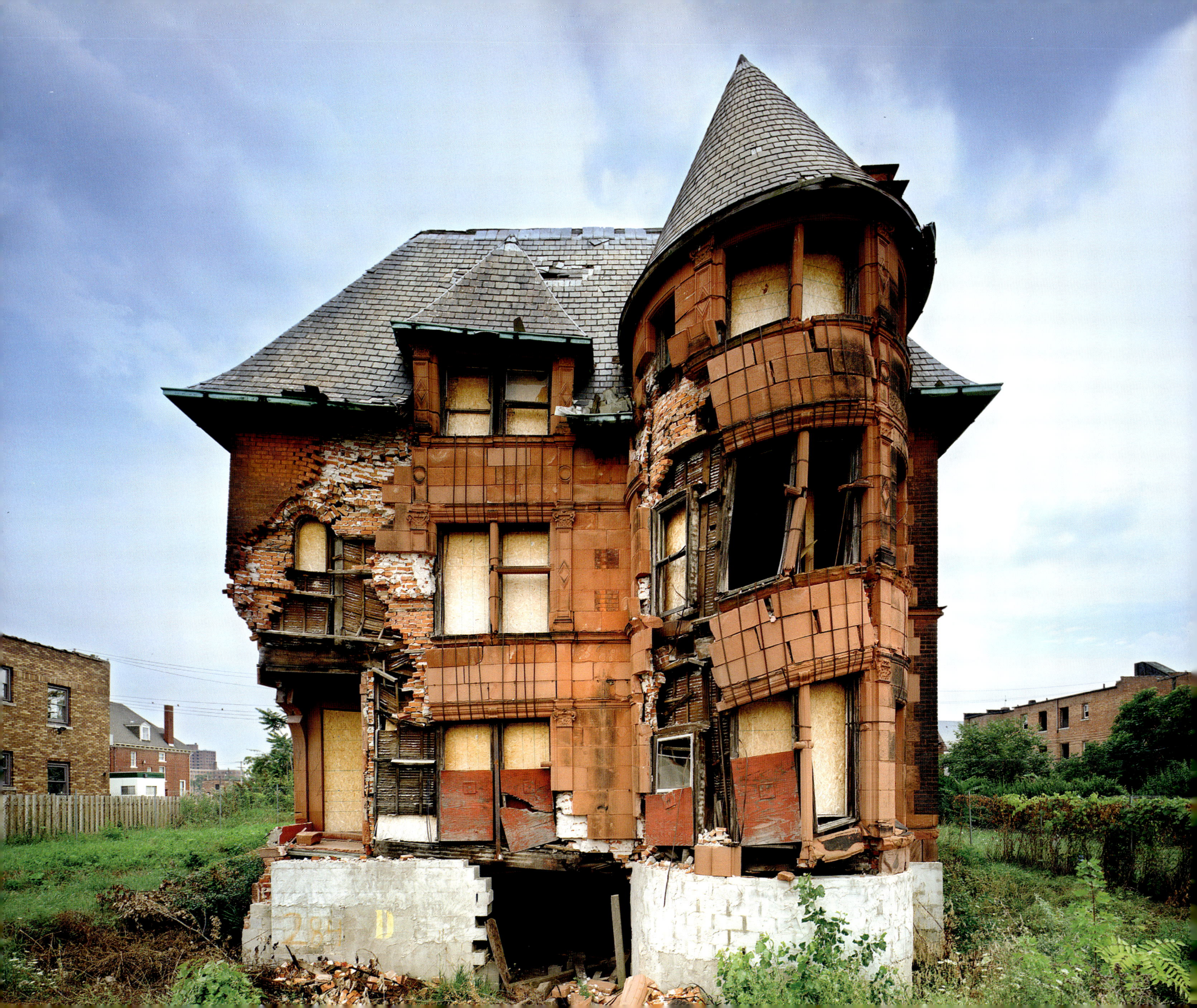

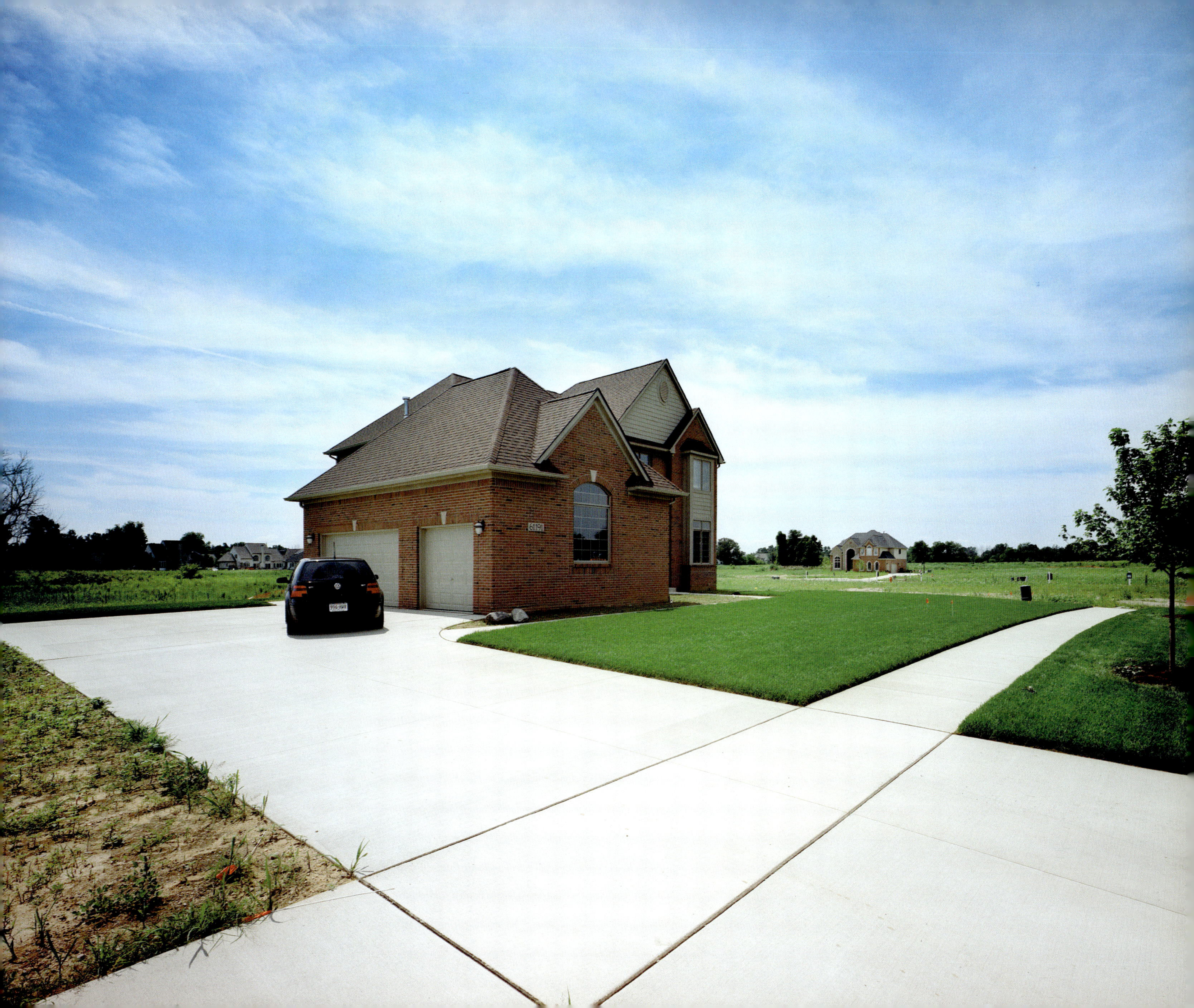

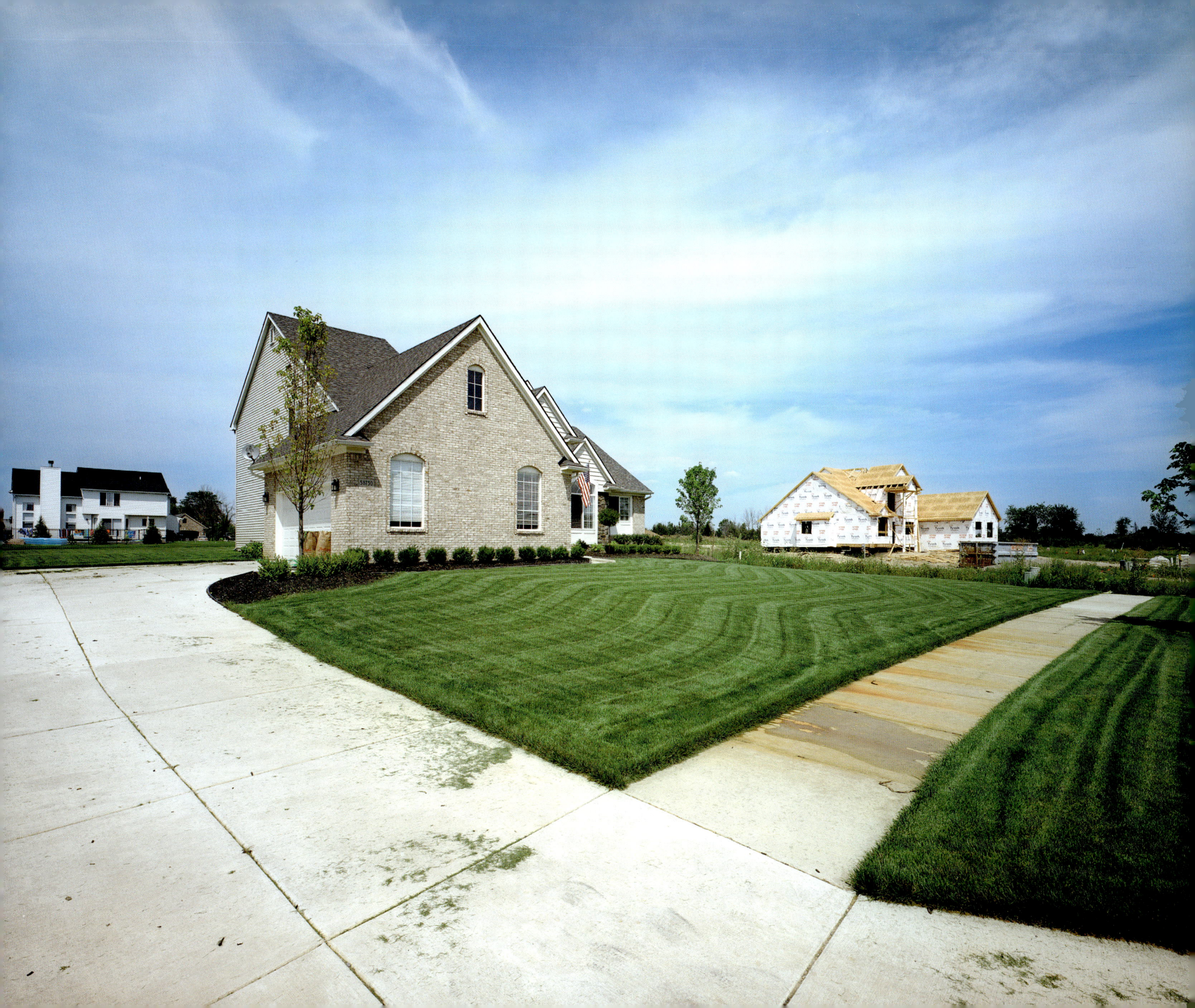

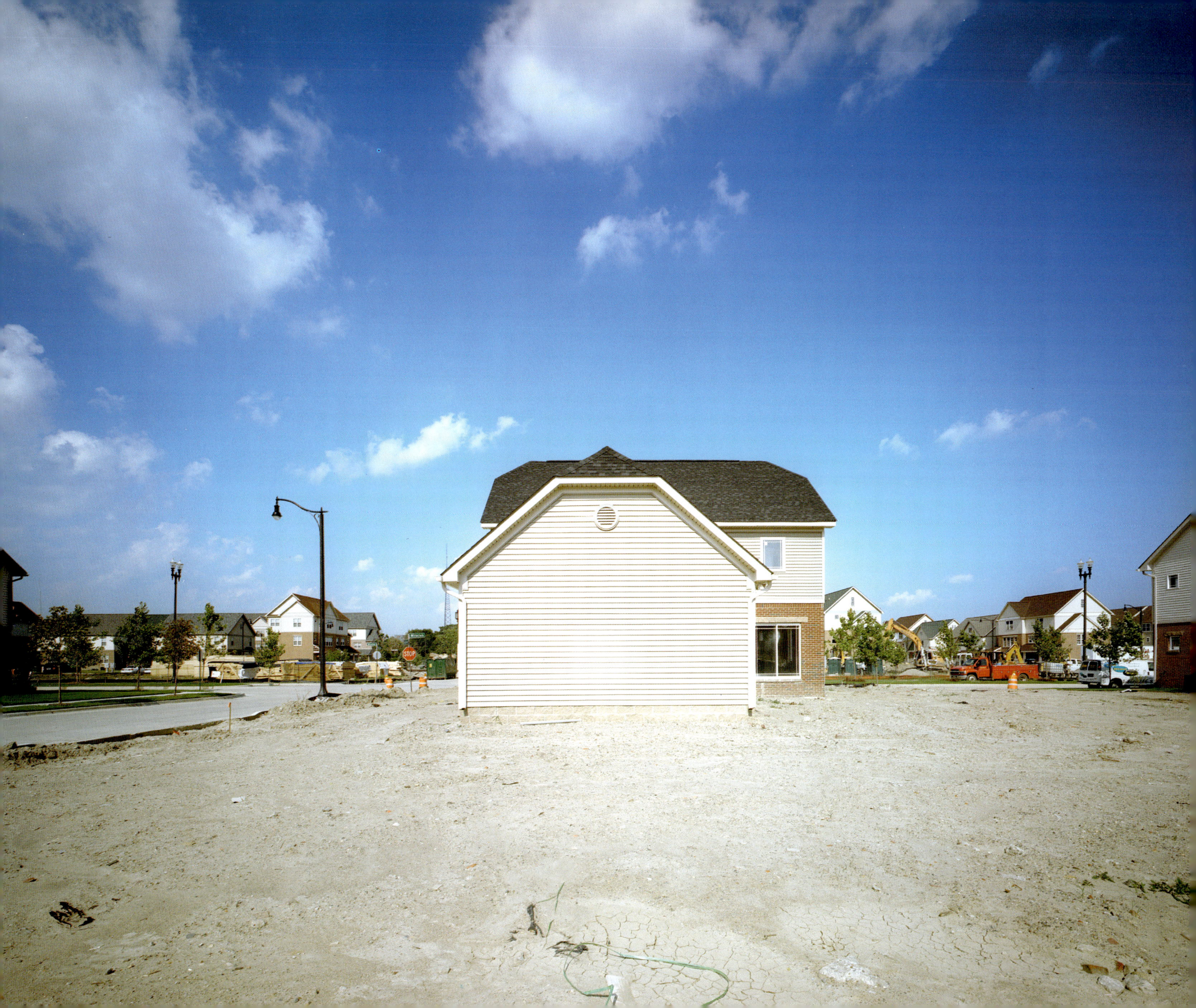

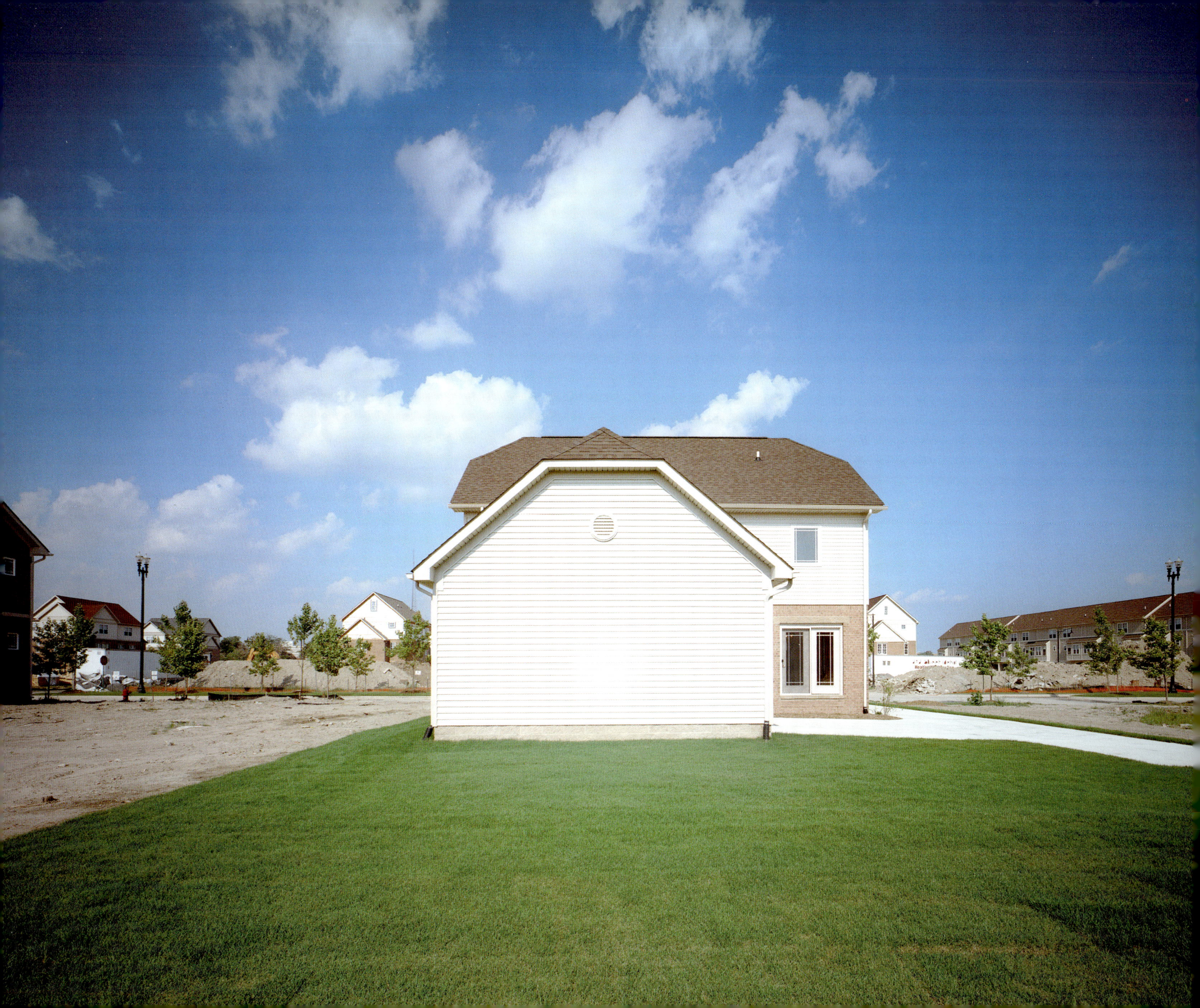

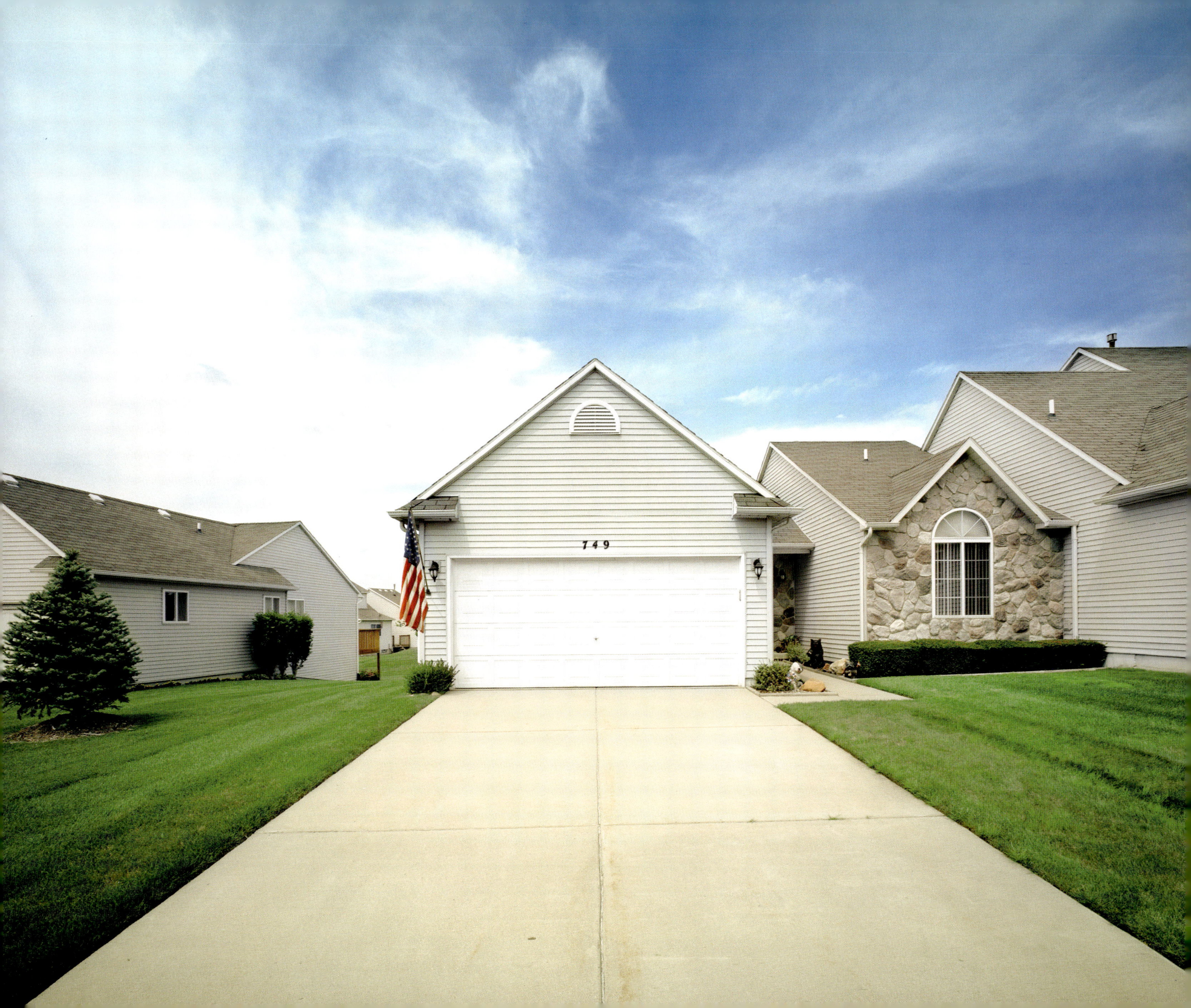

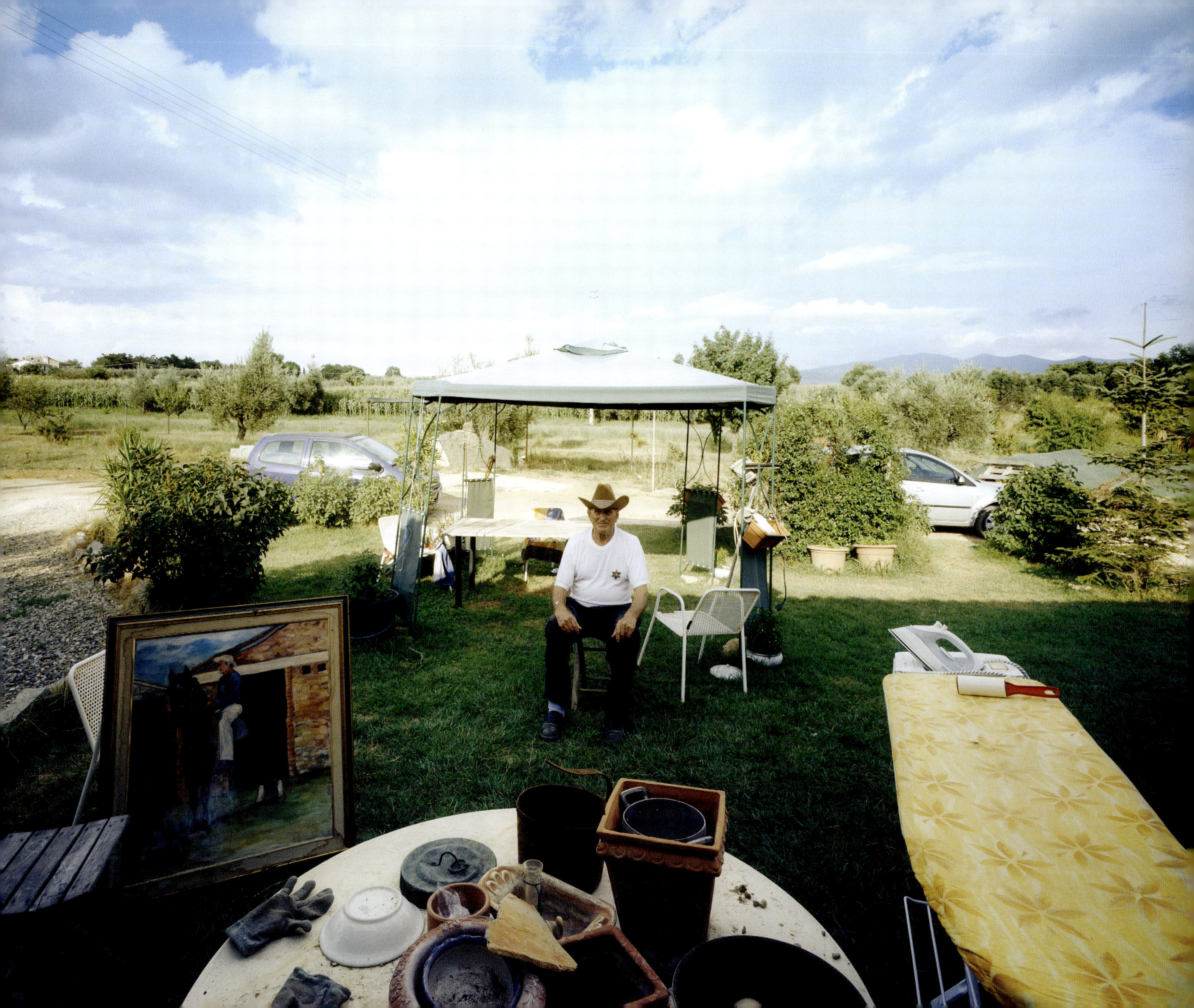

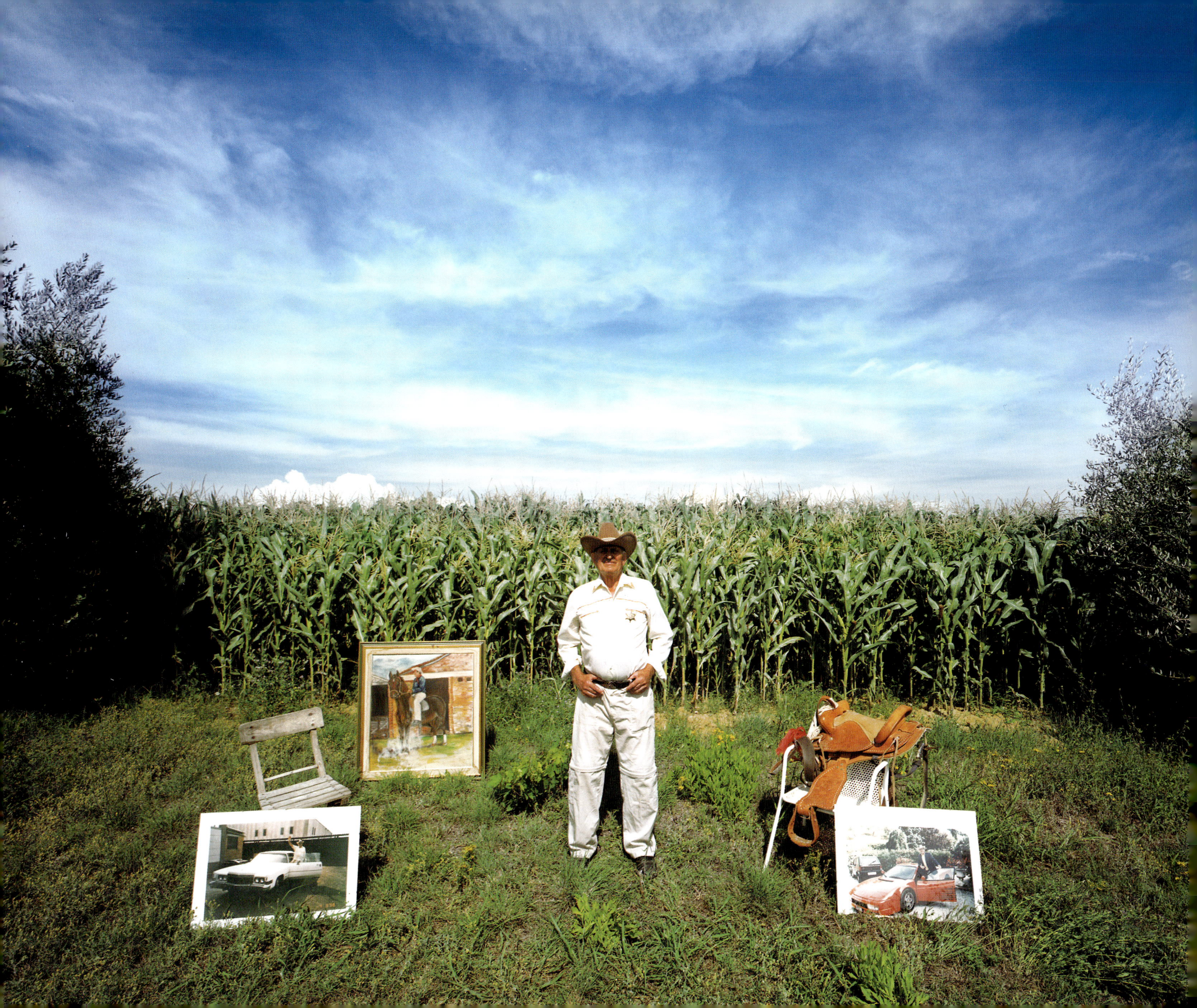

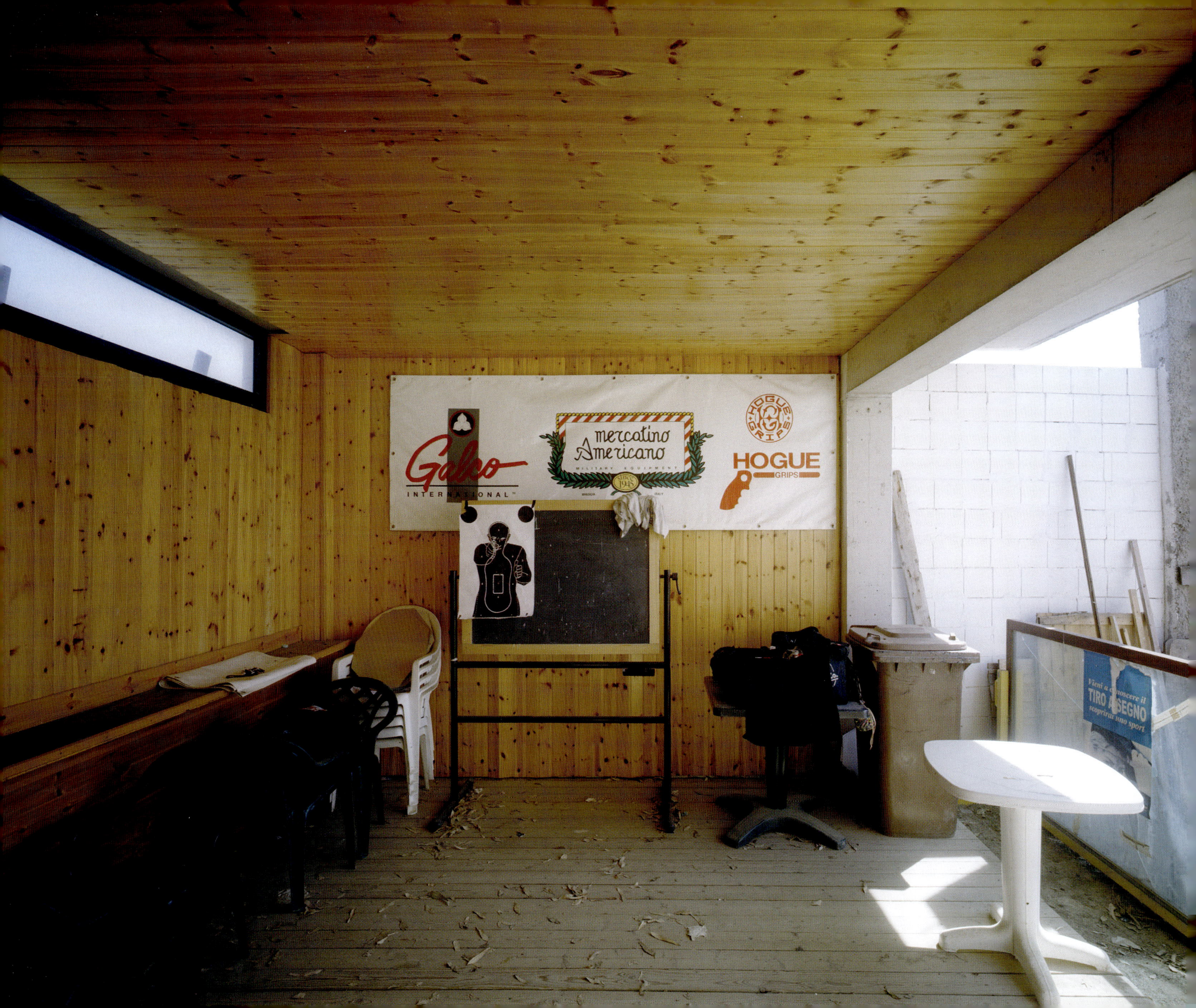
Galco
INTERNATIONAL
mercatino
Americano
MILITARY EQUIPMENT
SINCE 1945
BRESCIA   ITALY
HOGUE
GRIPS
HOGUE
GRIPS
Vieni a conoscere il
TIRO A SEGNO
scoprirai uno sport

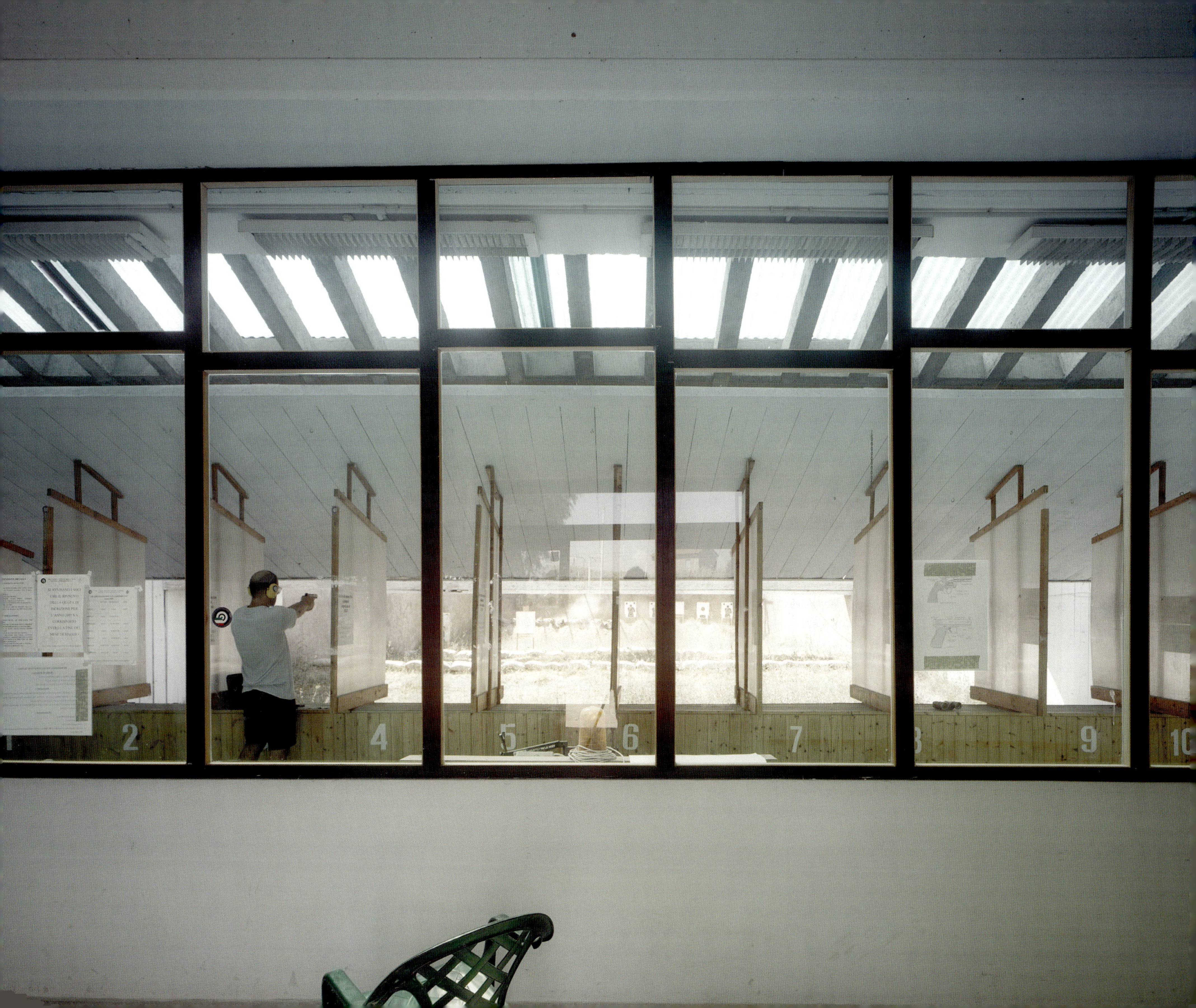

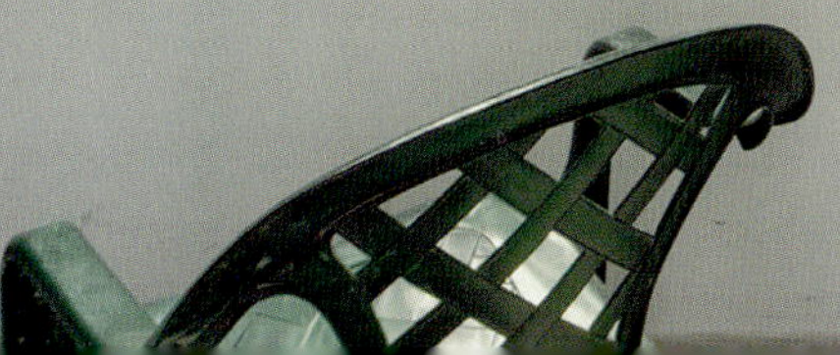

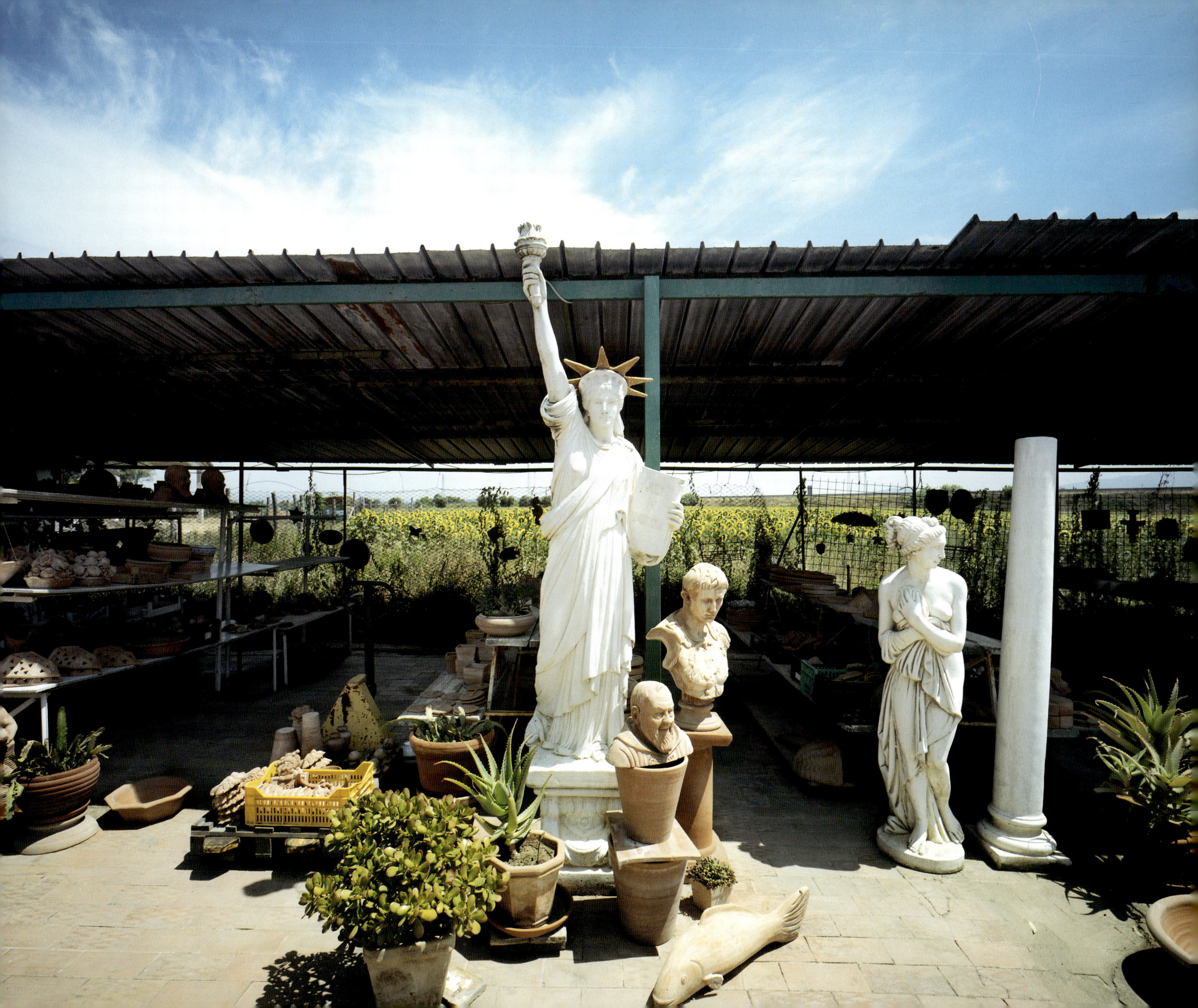

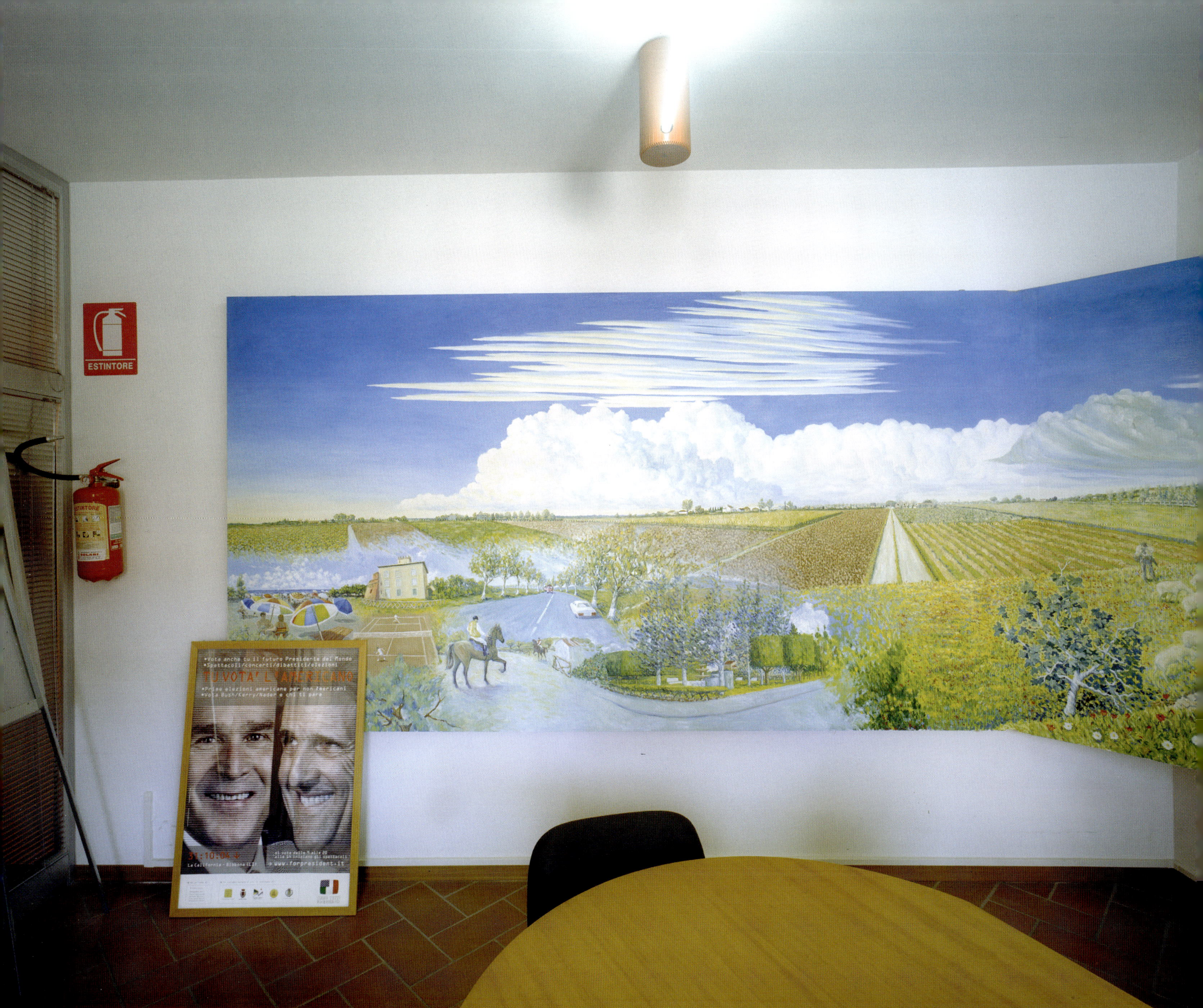

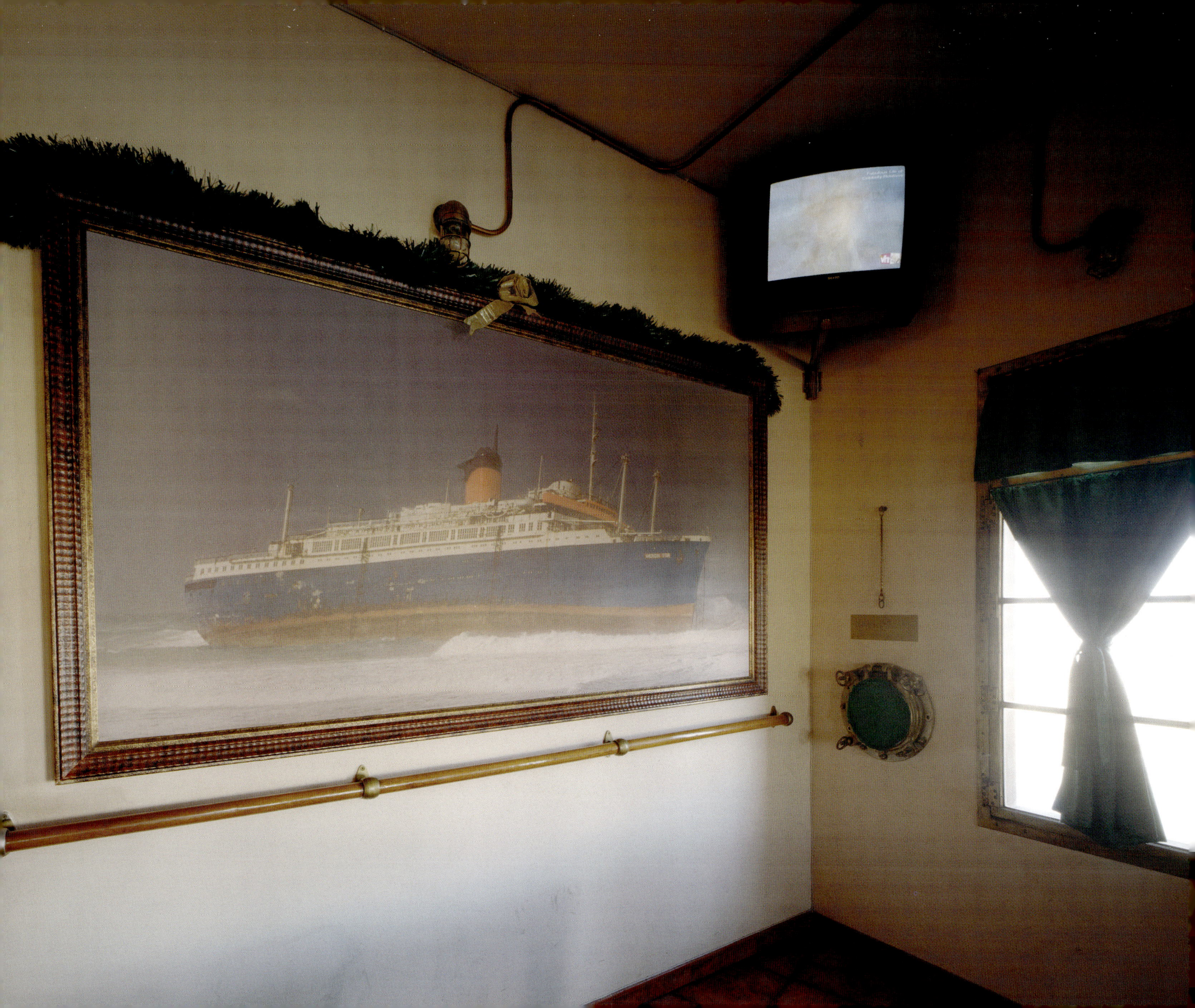

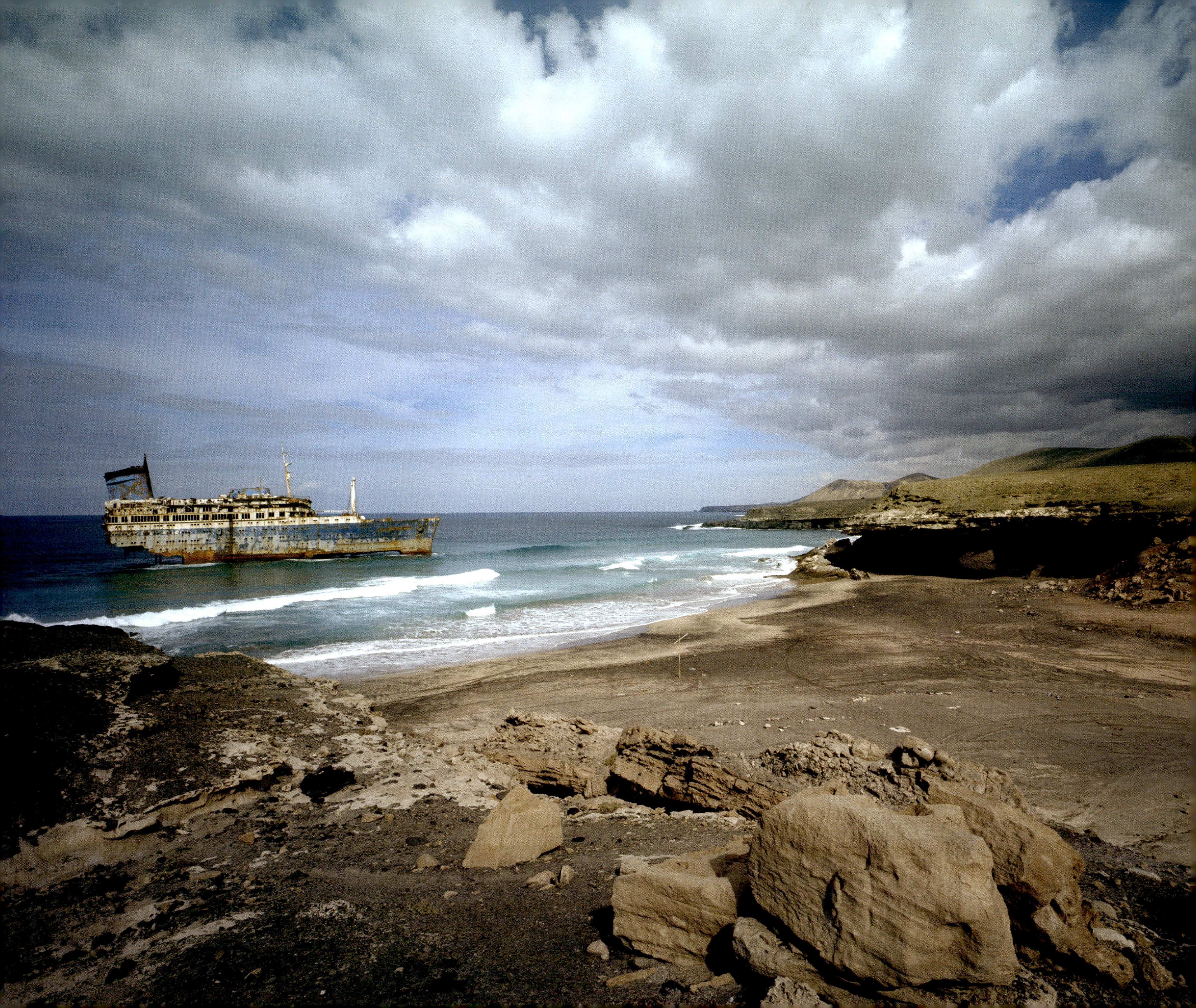

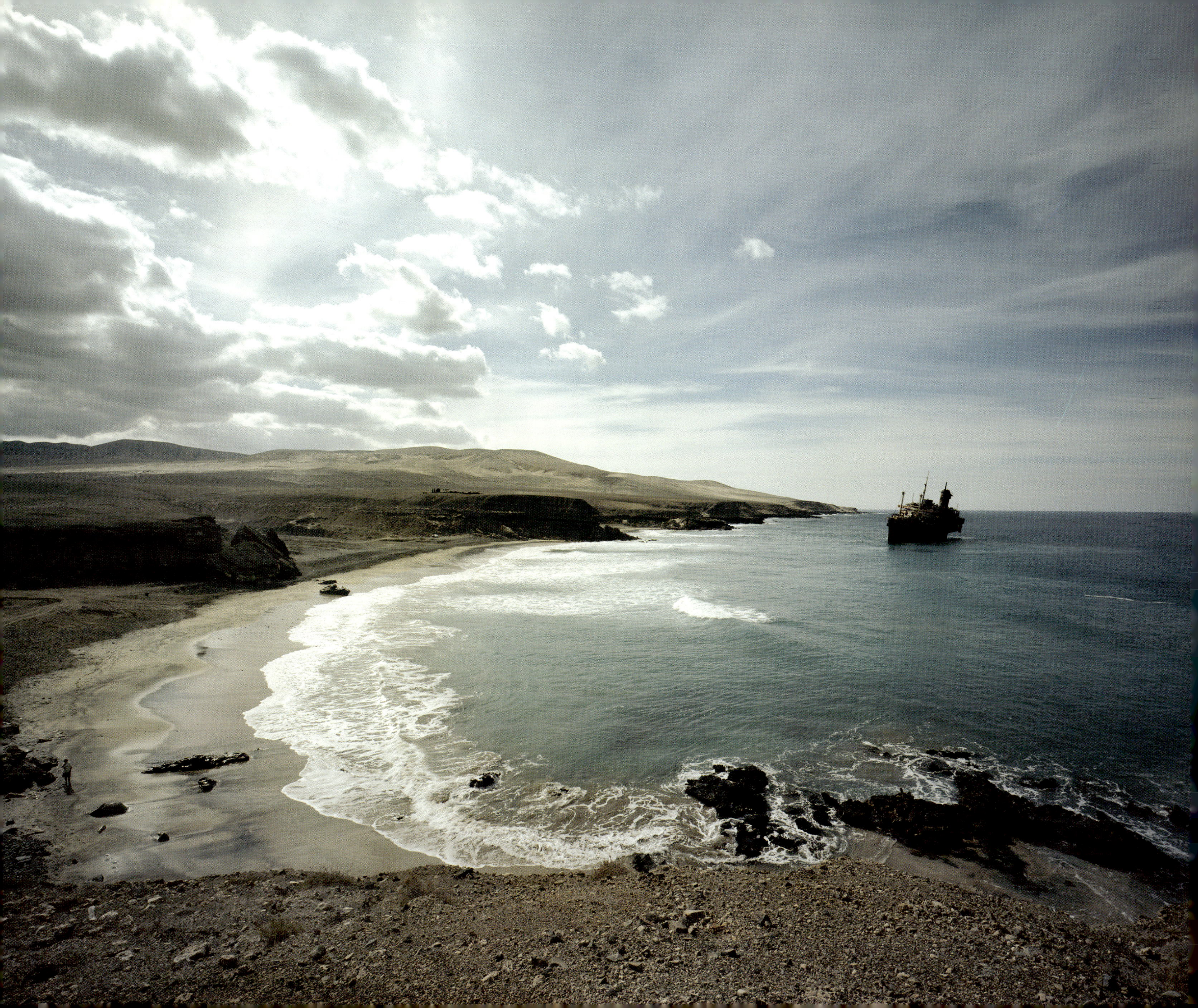

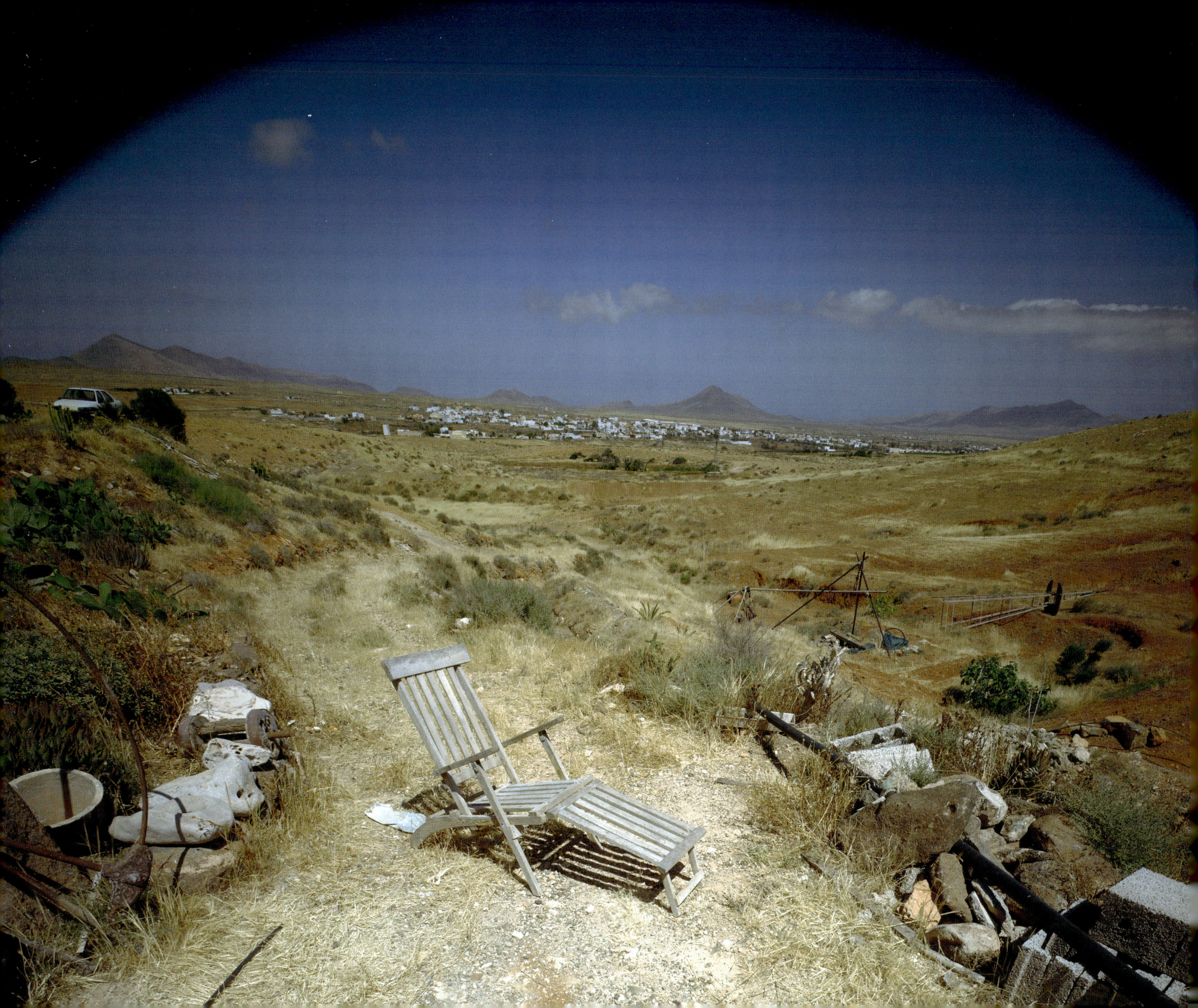

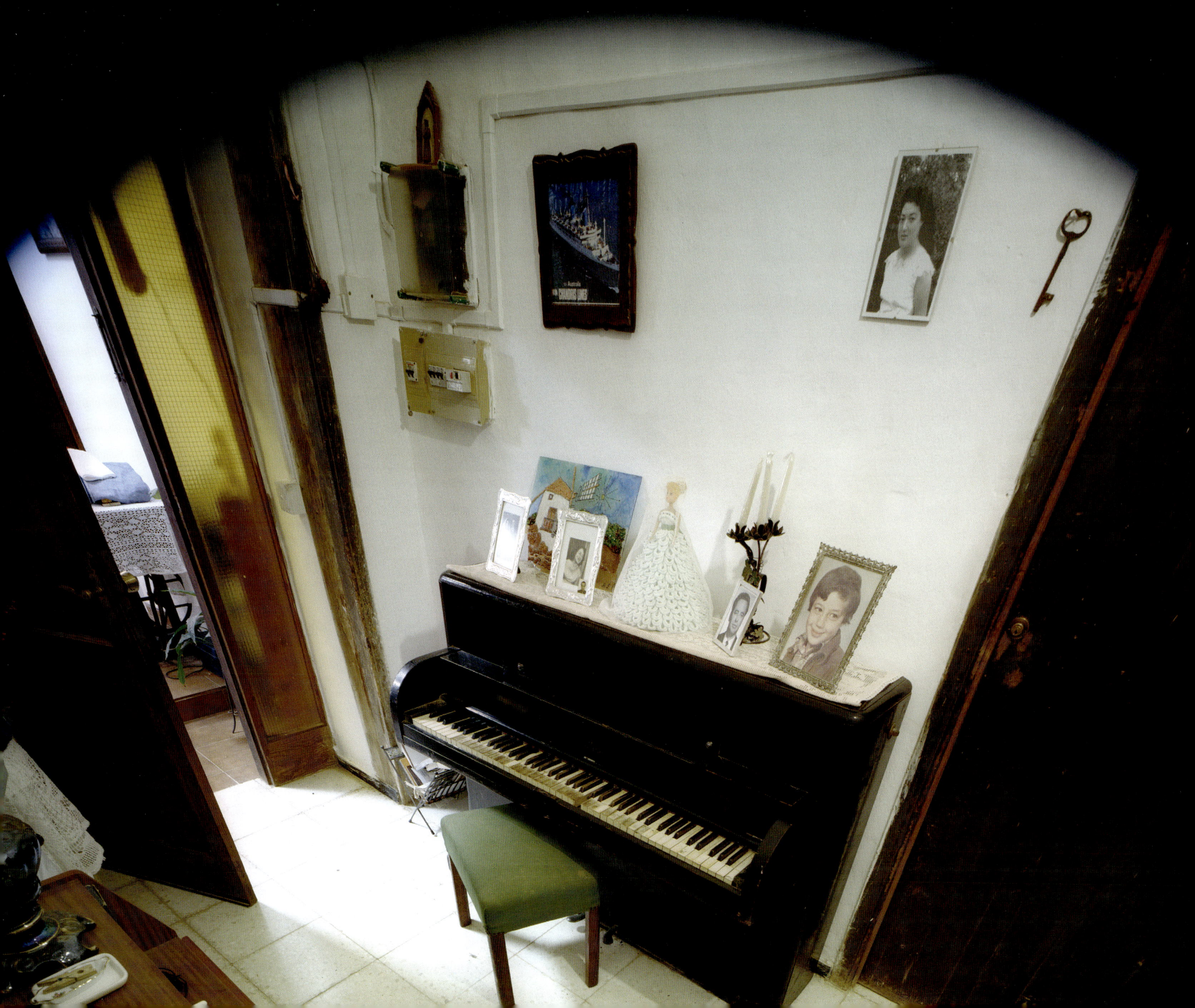

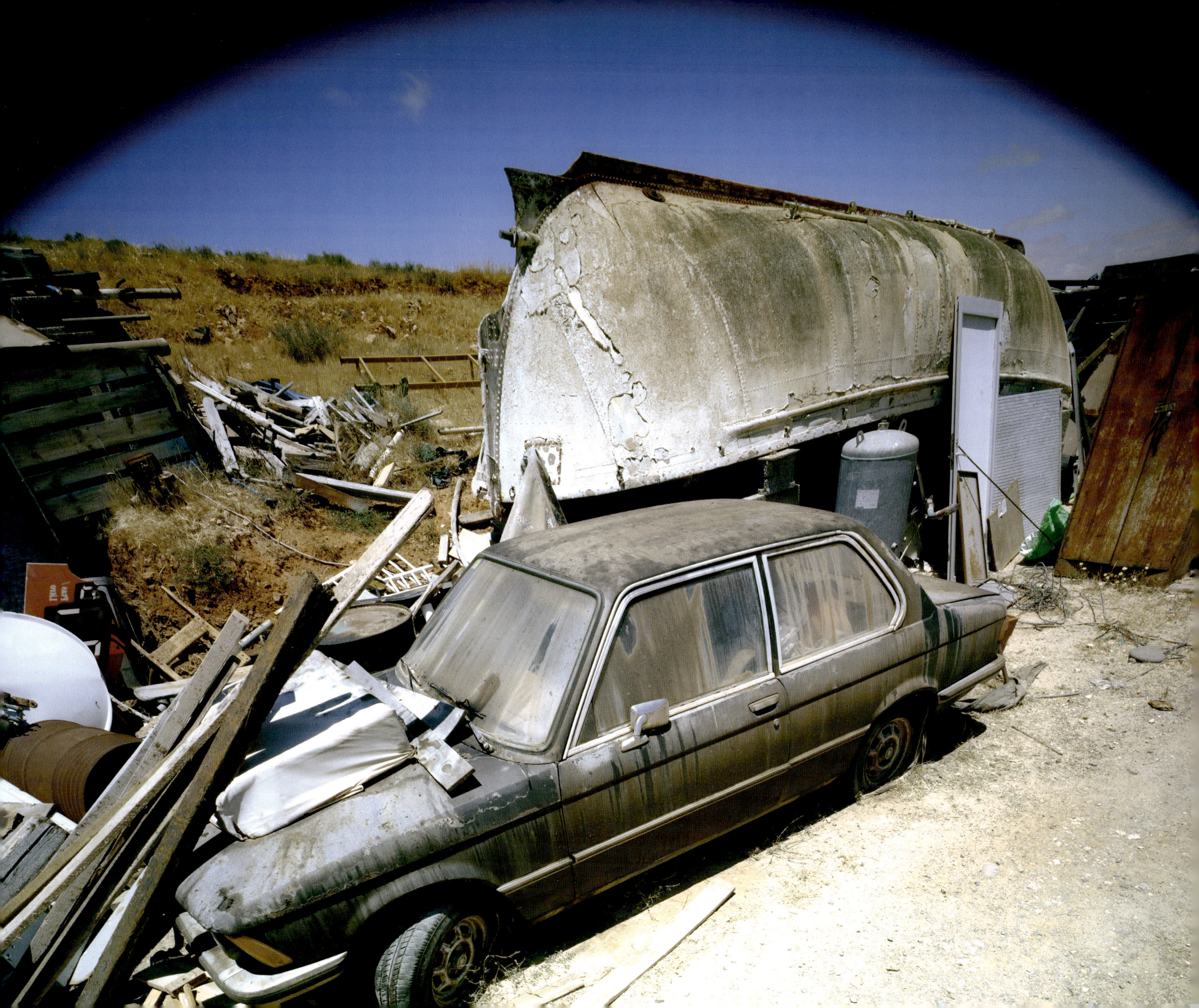

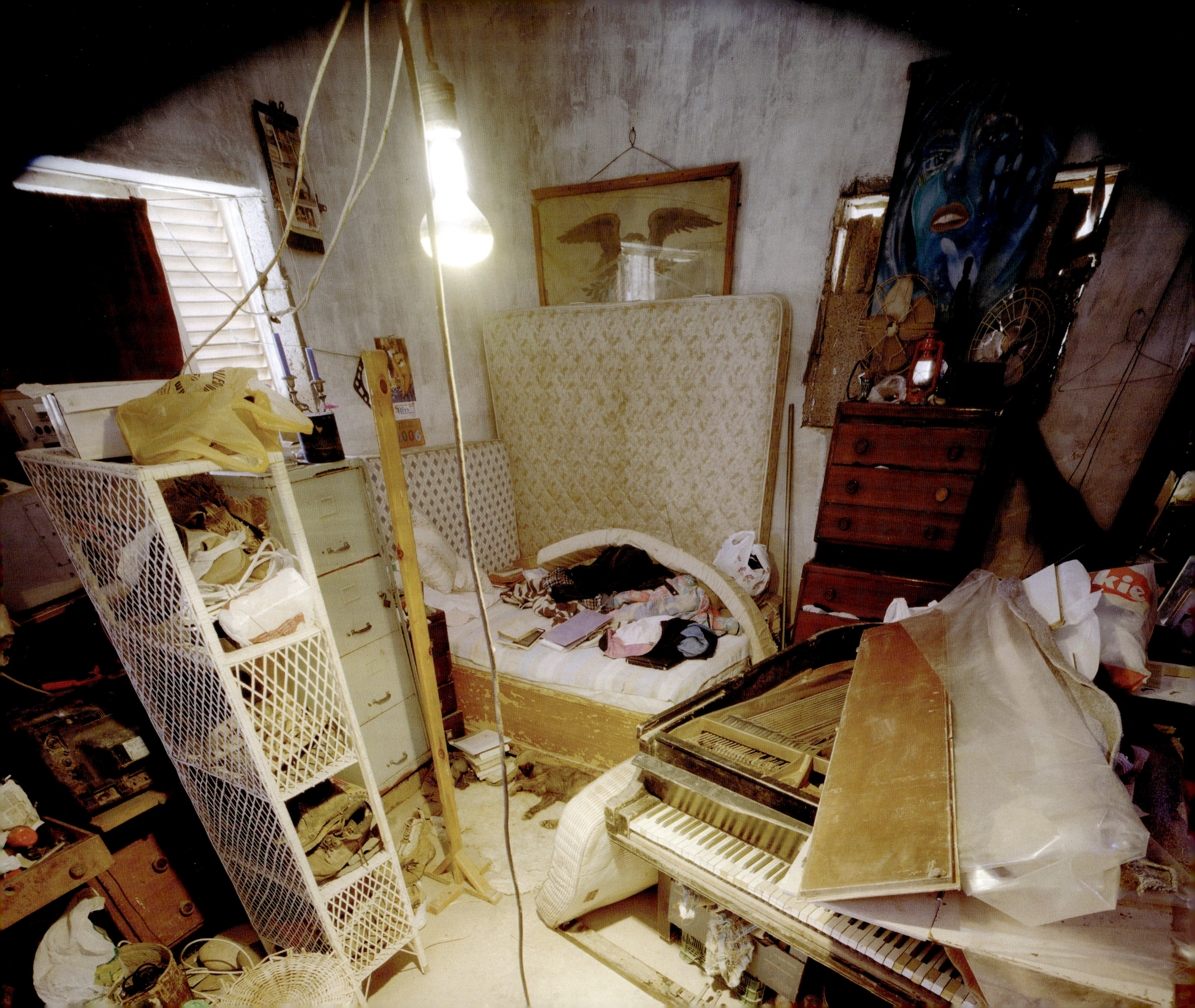

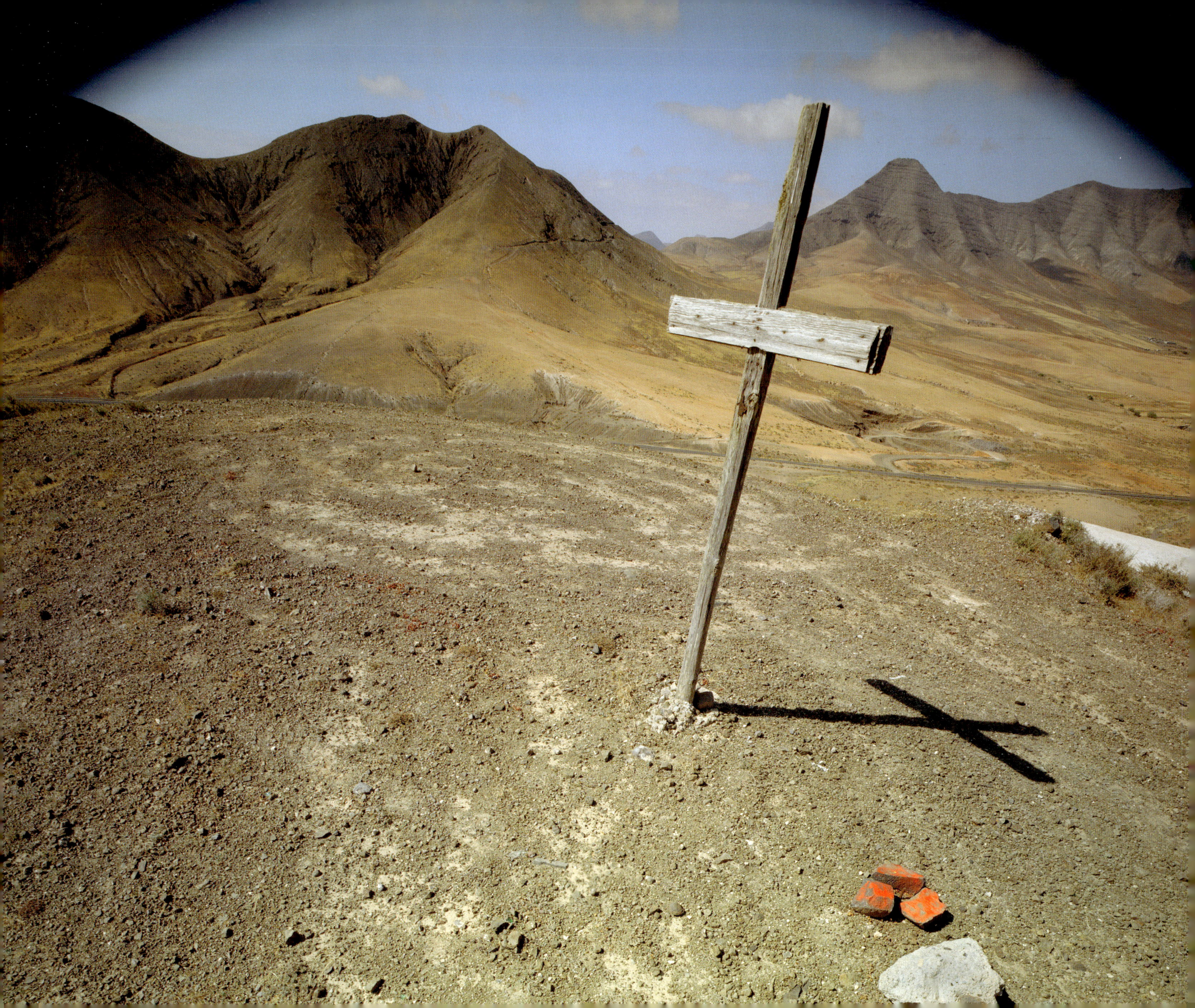

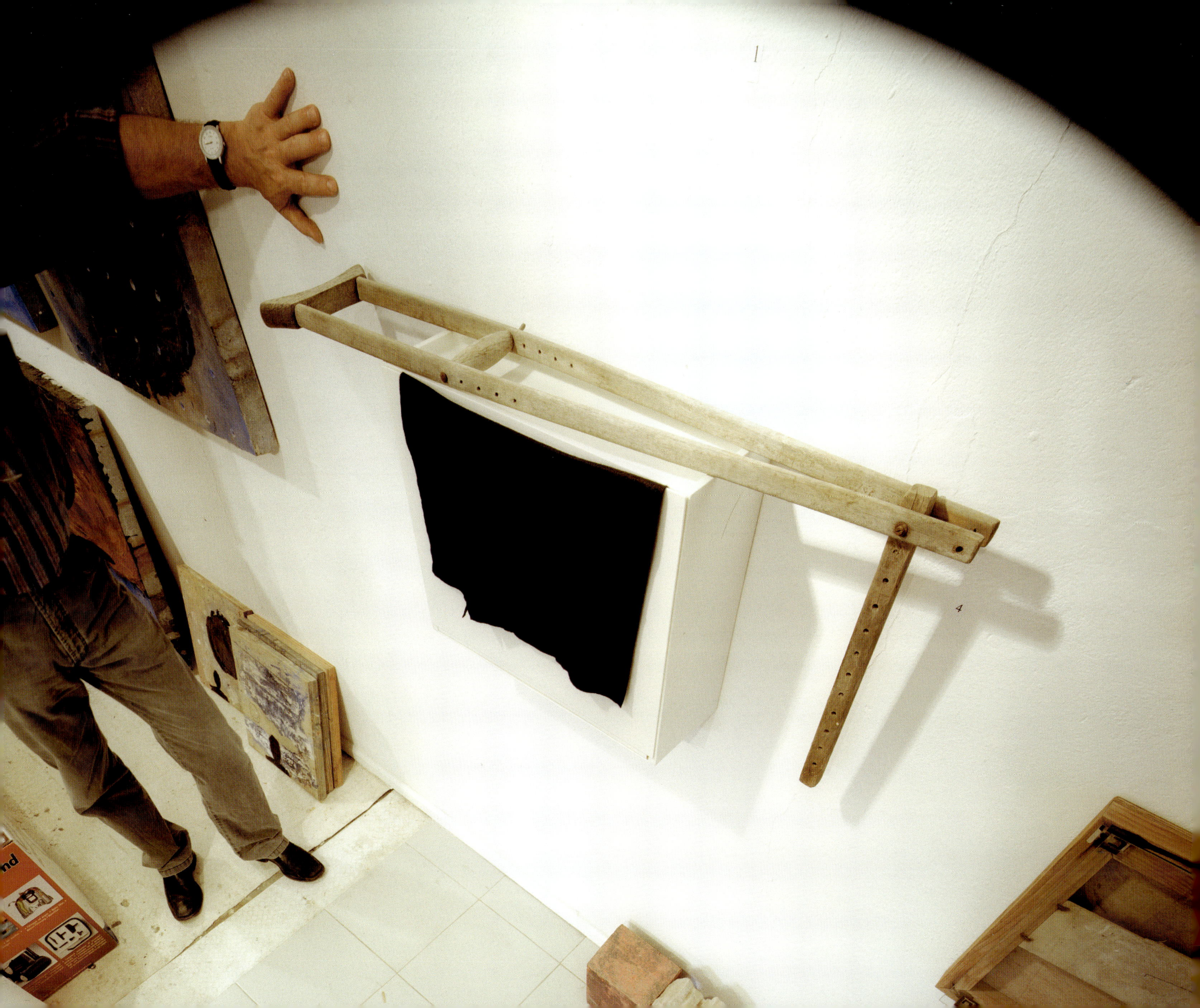

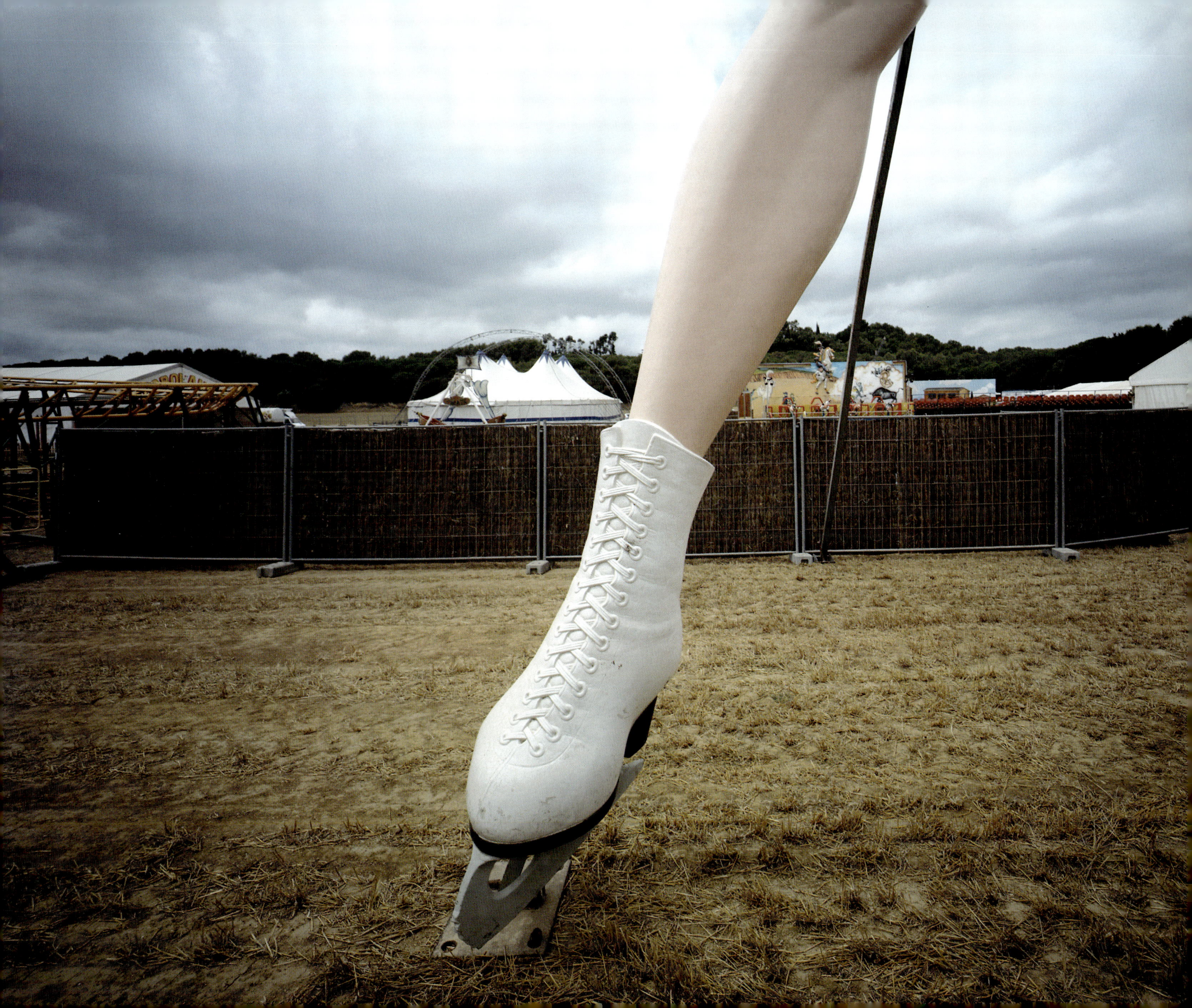

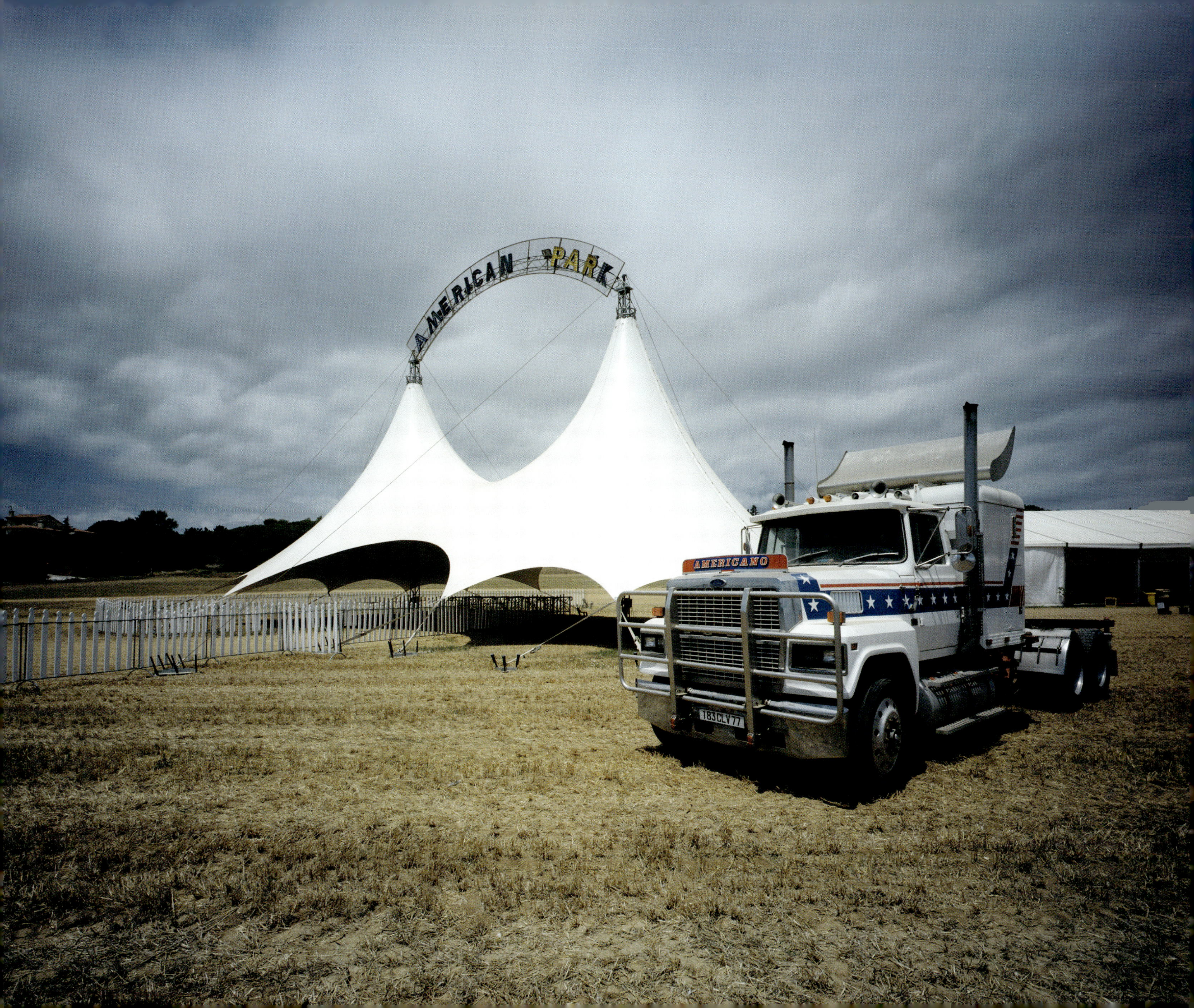
AMERICAN PARK
AMERICANO
183 CLV 77

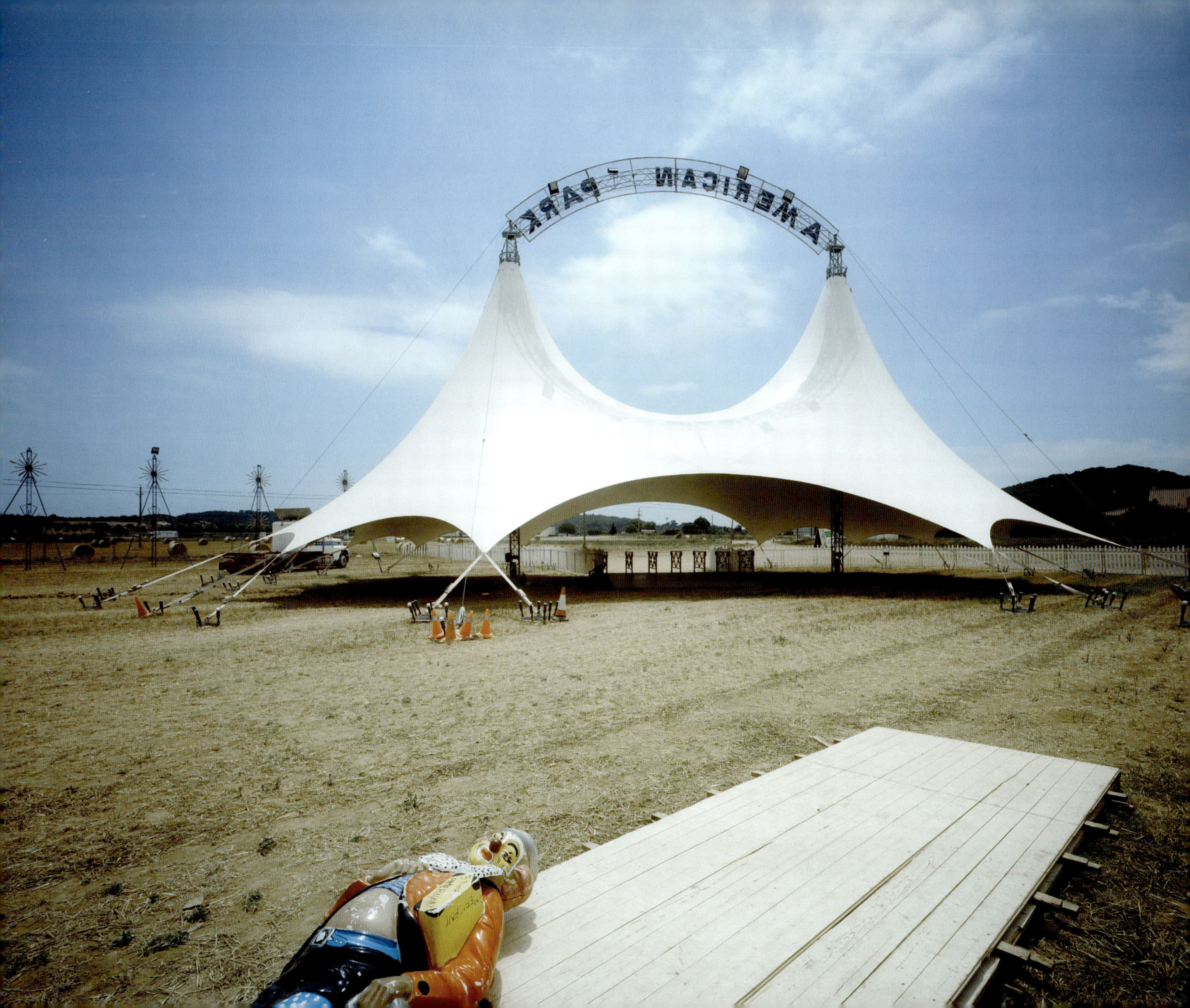
AMERICAN · PARK

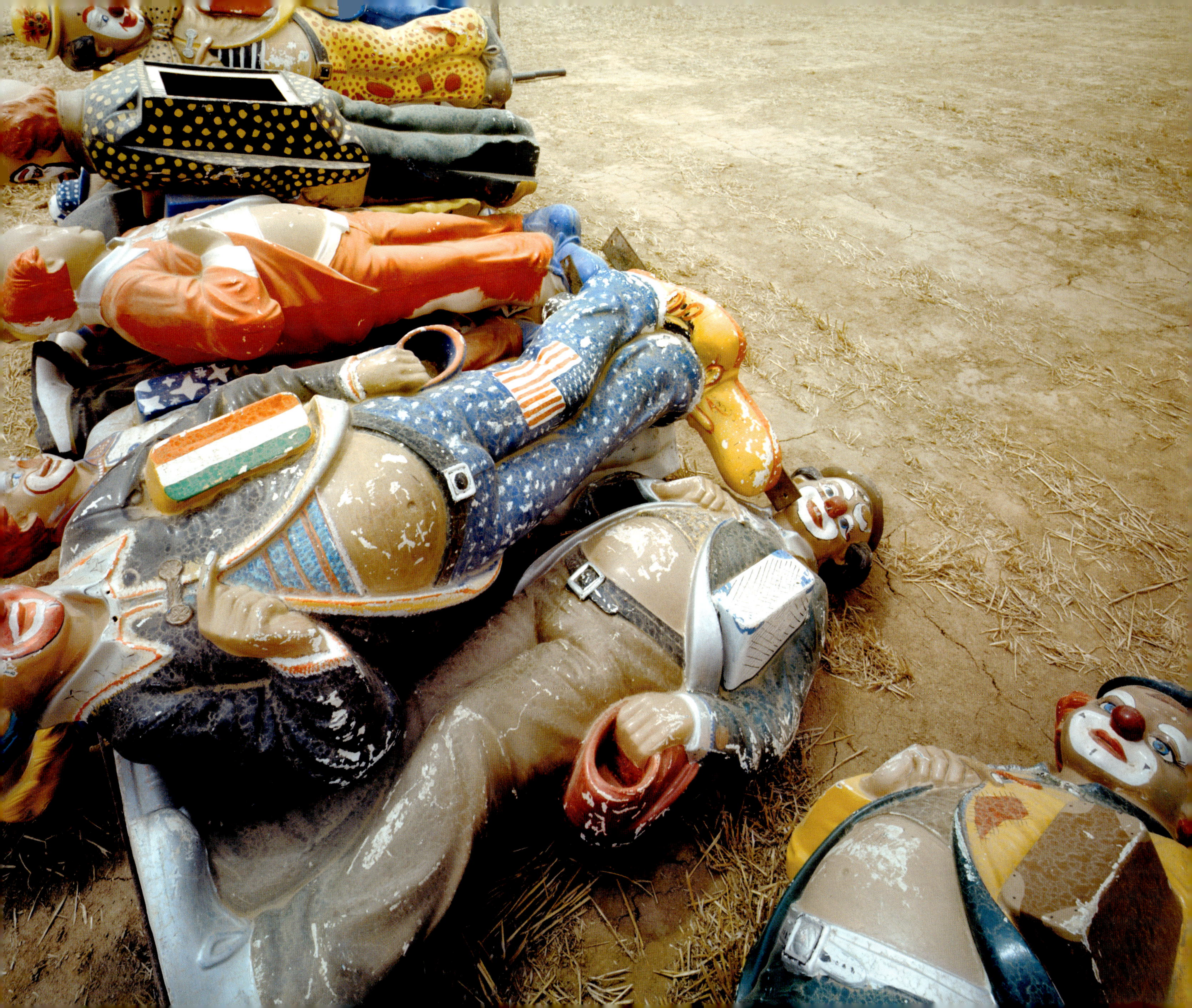

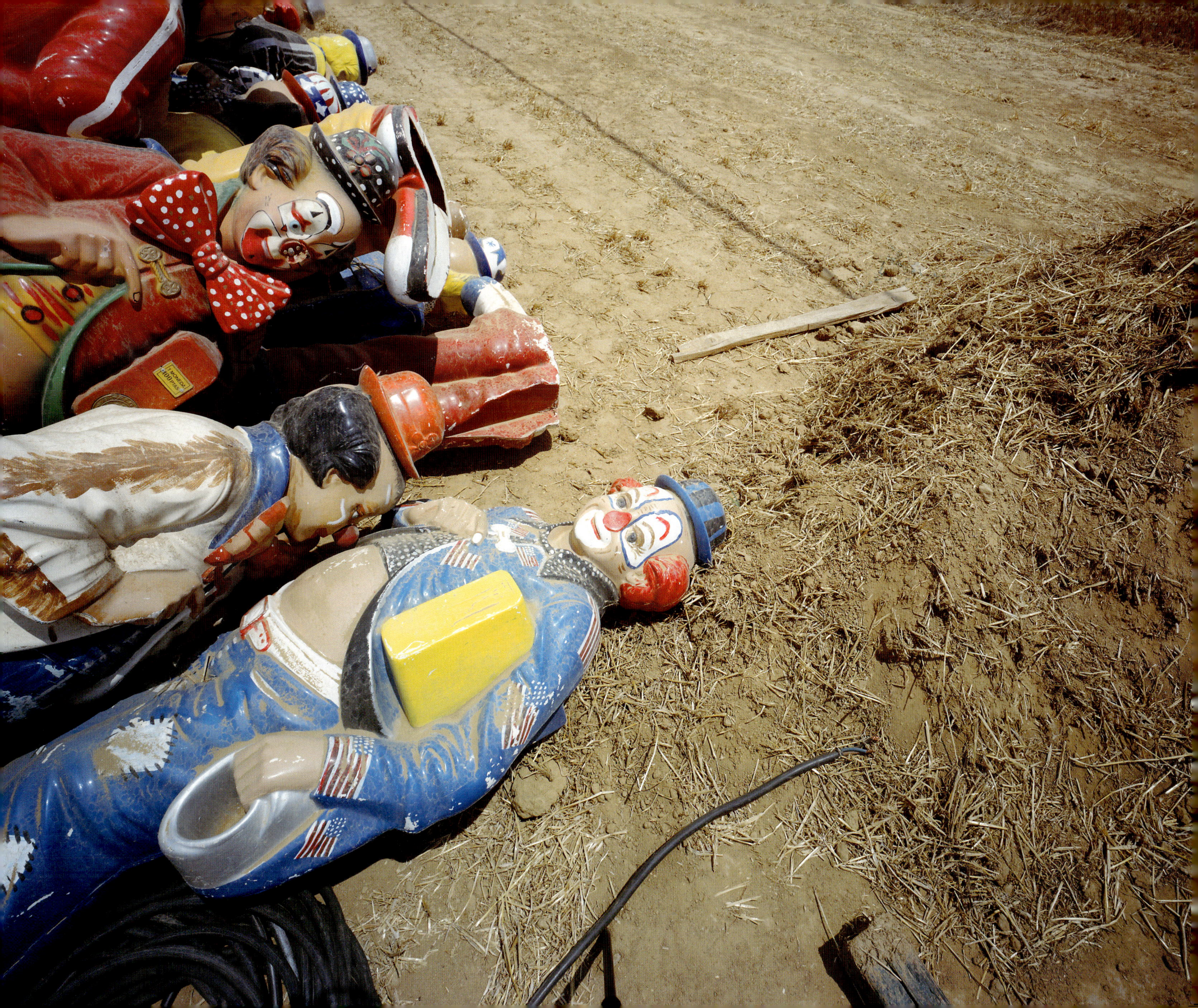

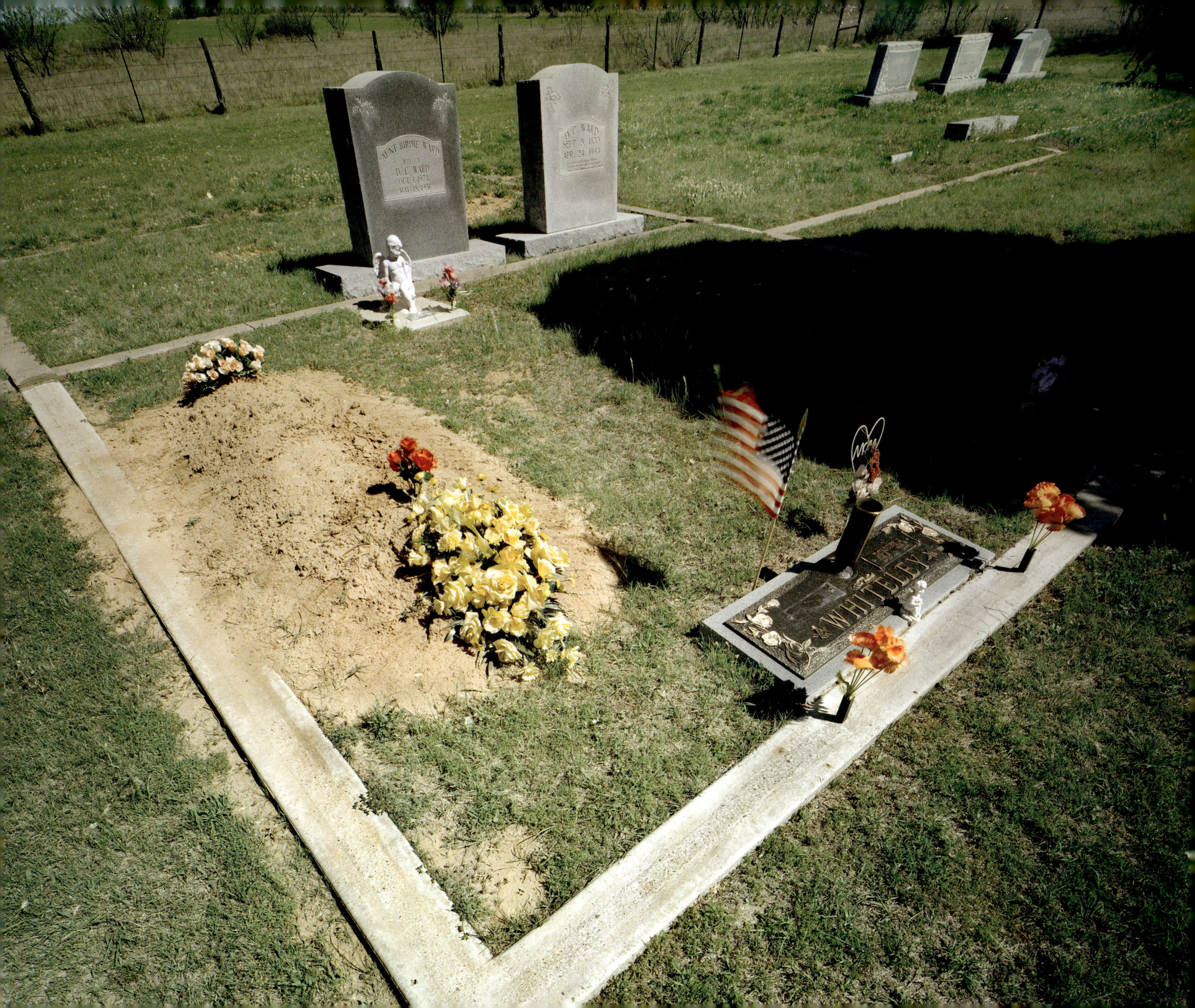

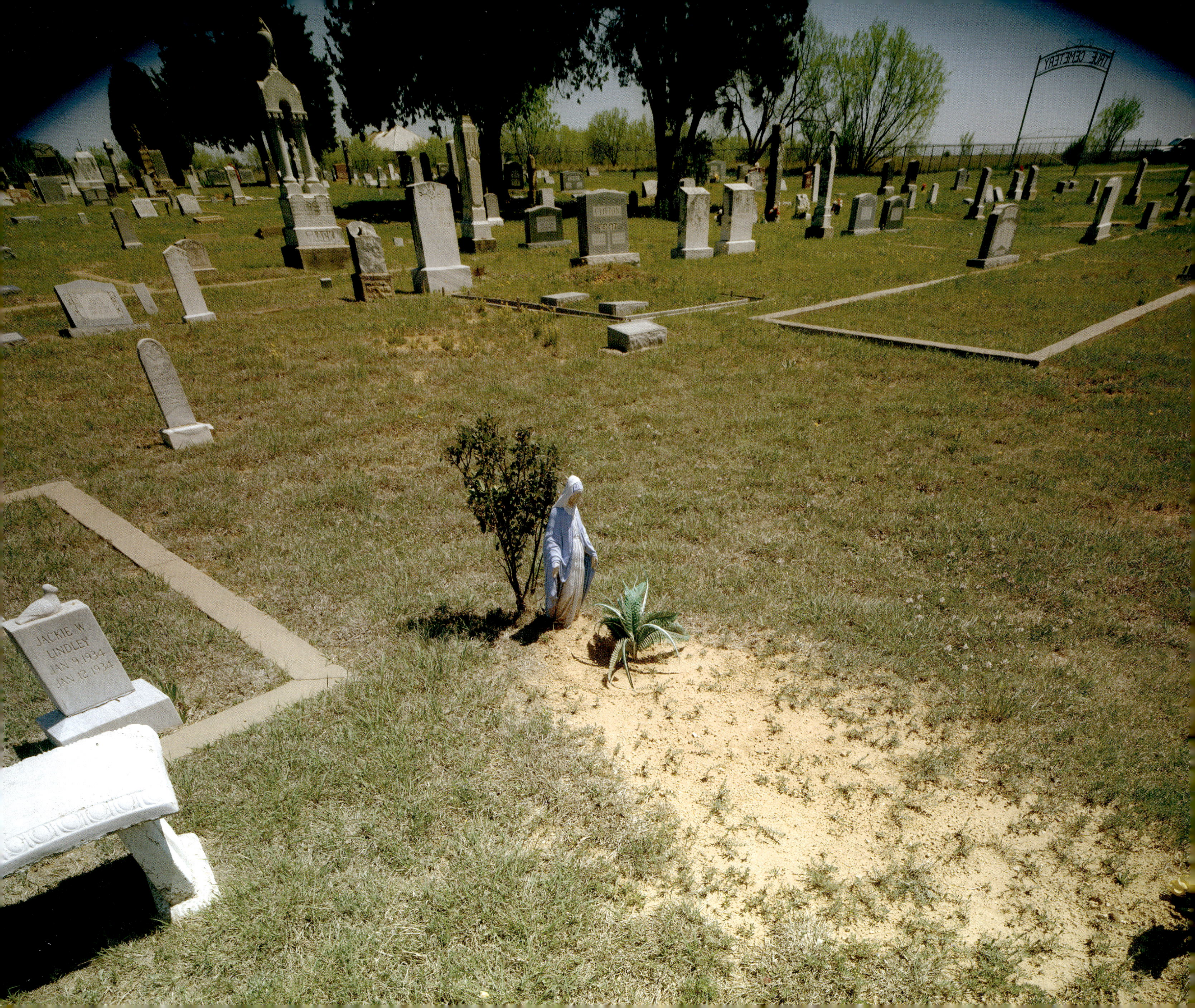
JACKIE W.
LINDLEY
JAN 9 1934
JAN 12 1934
TRUE CEMETERY

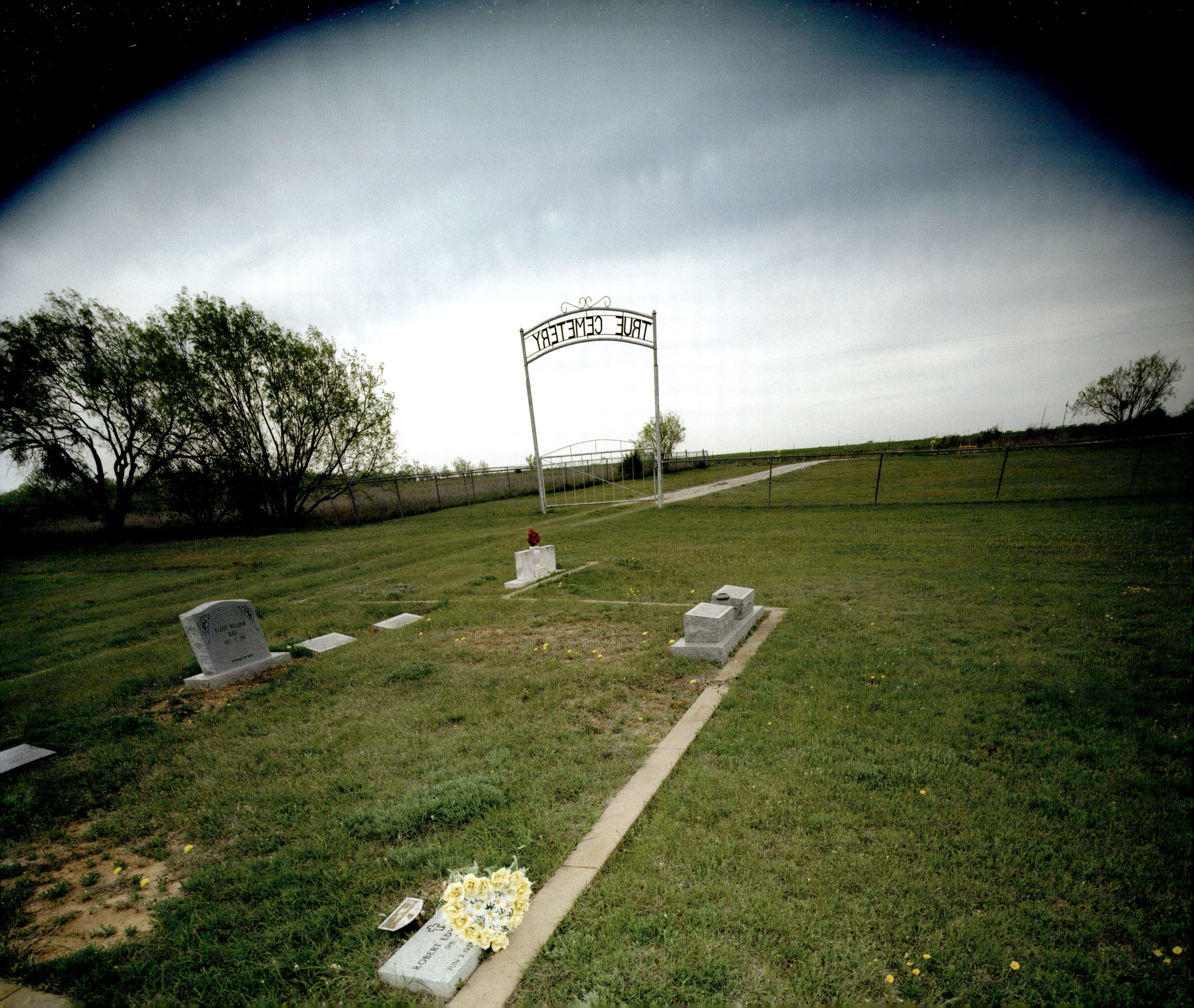
TRUE CEMETERY

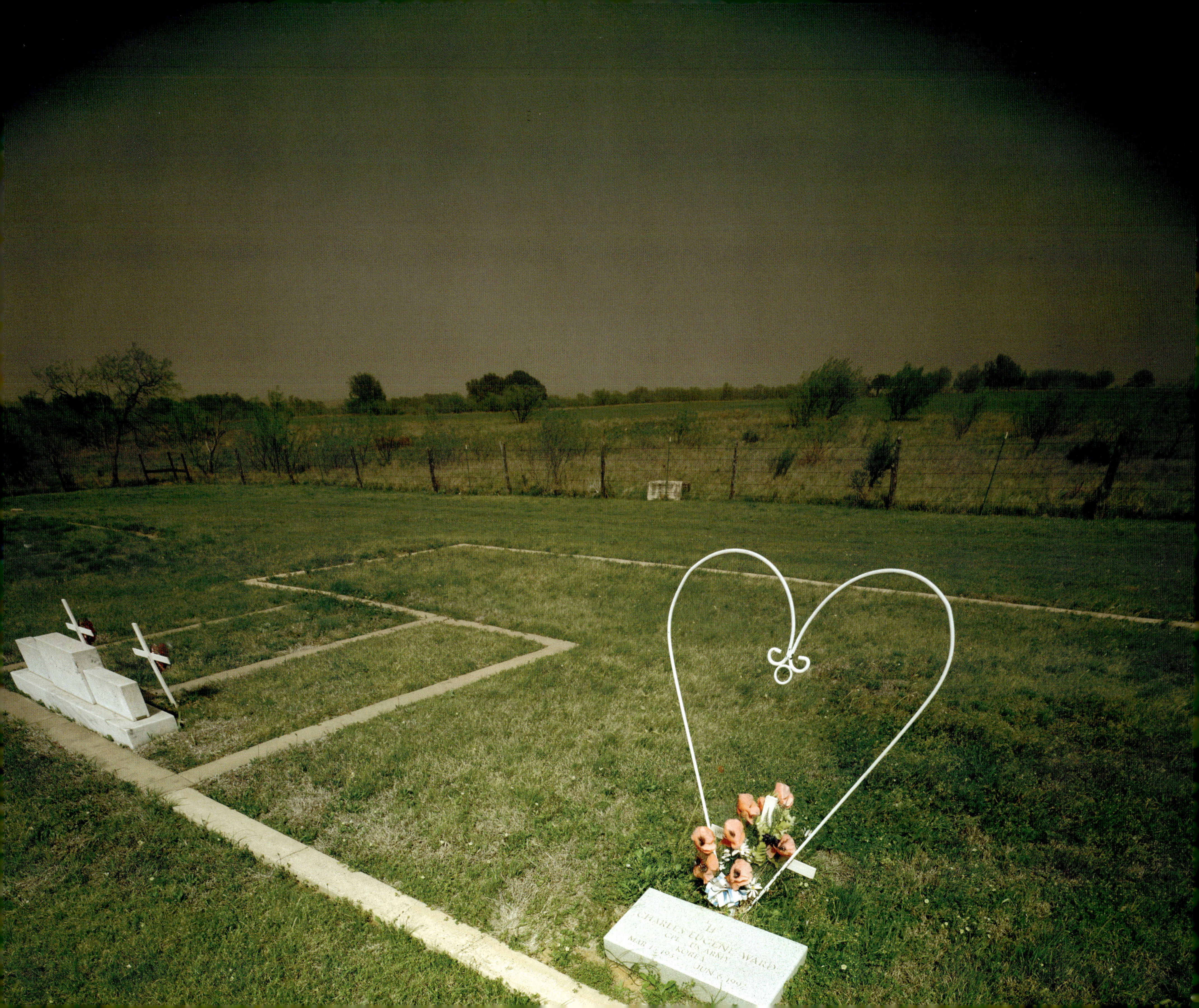
CHARLEY EUGENE WARD
CPL US ARMY
KOREA
MAR 1 1933   JUN 8 1992

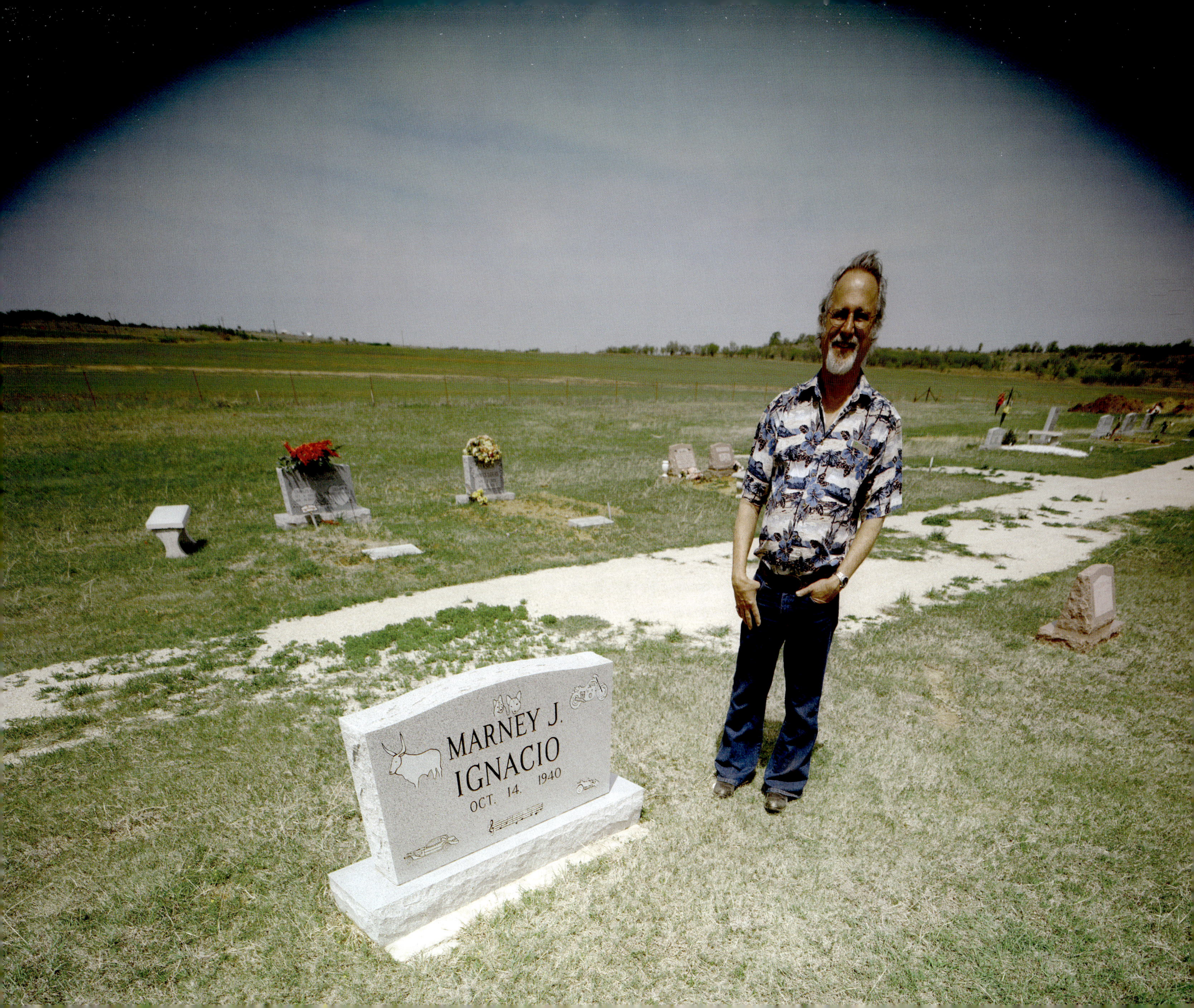

MARNEY J.
IGNACIO
OCT. 14, 1940

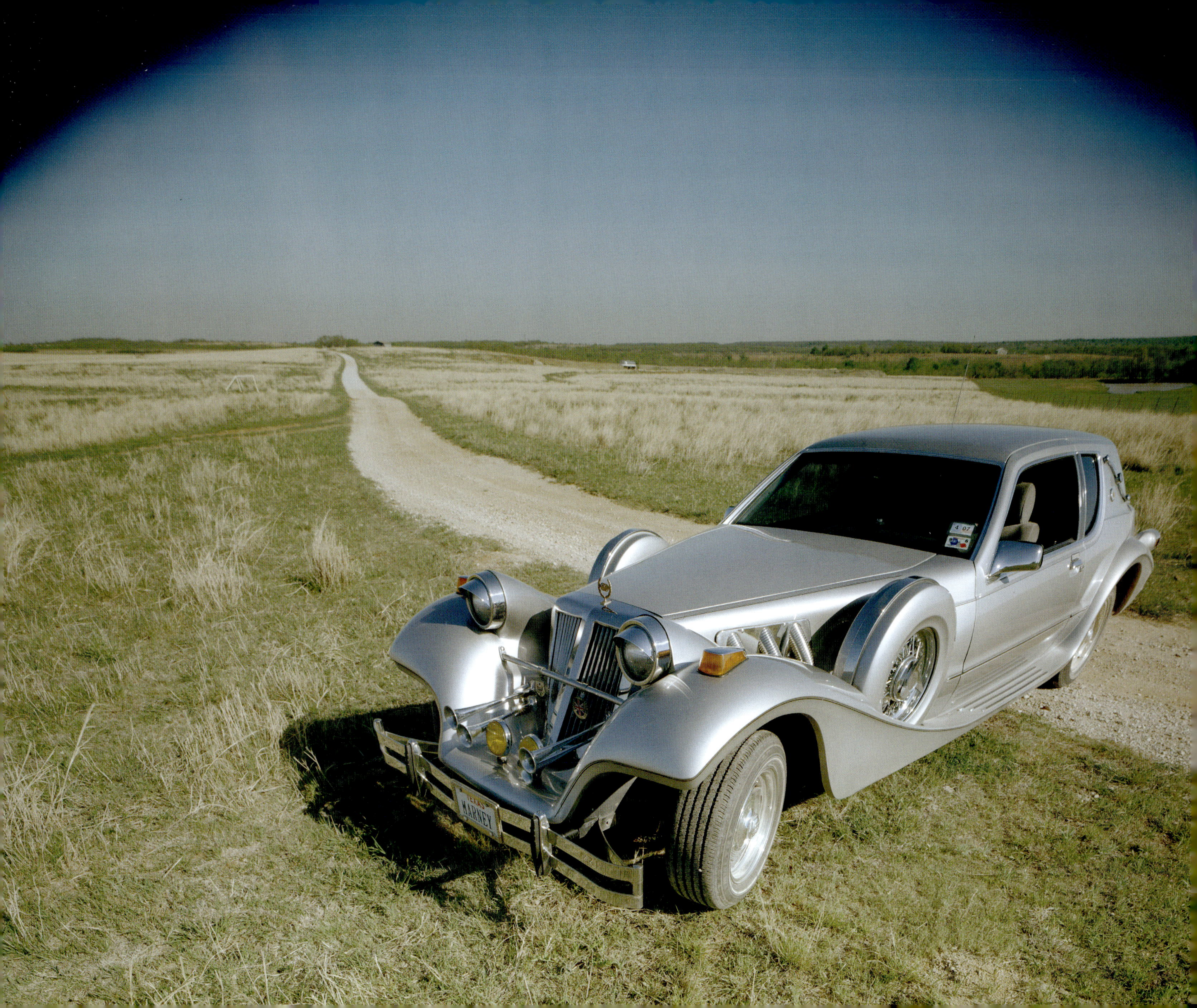

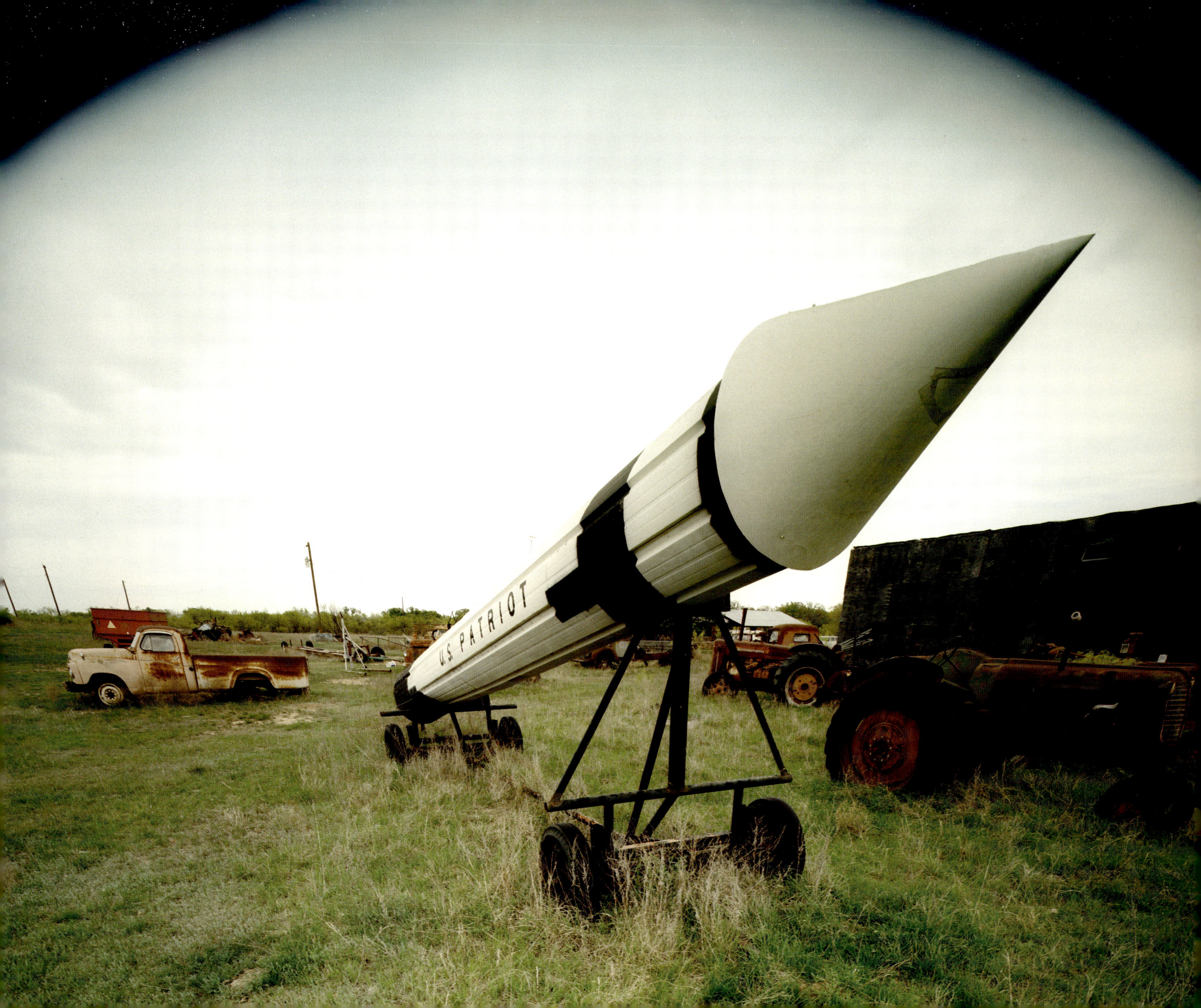
U.S. PATRIOT

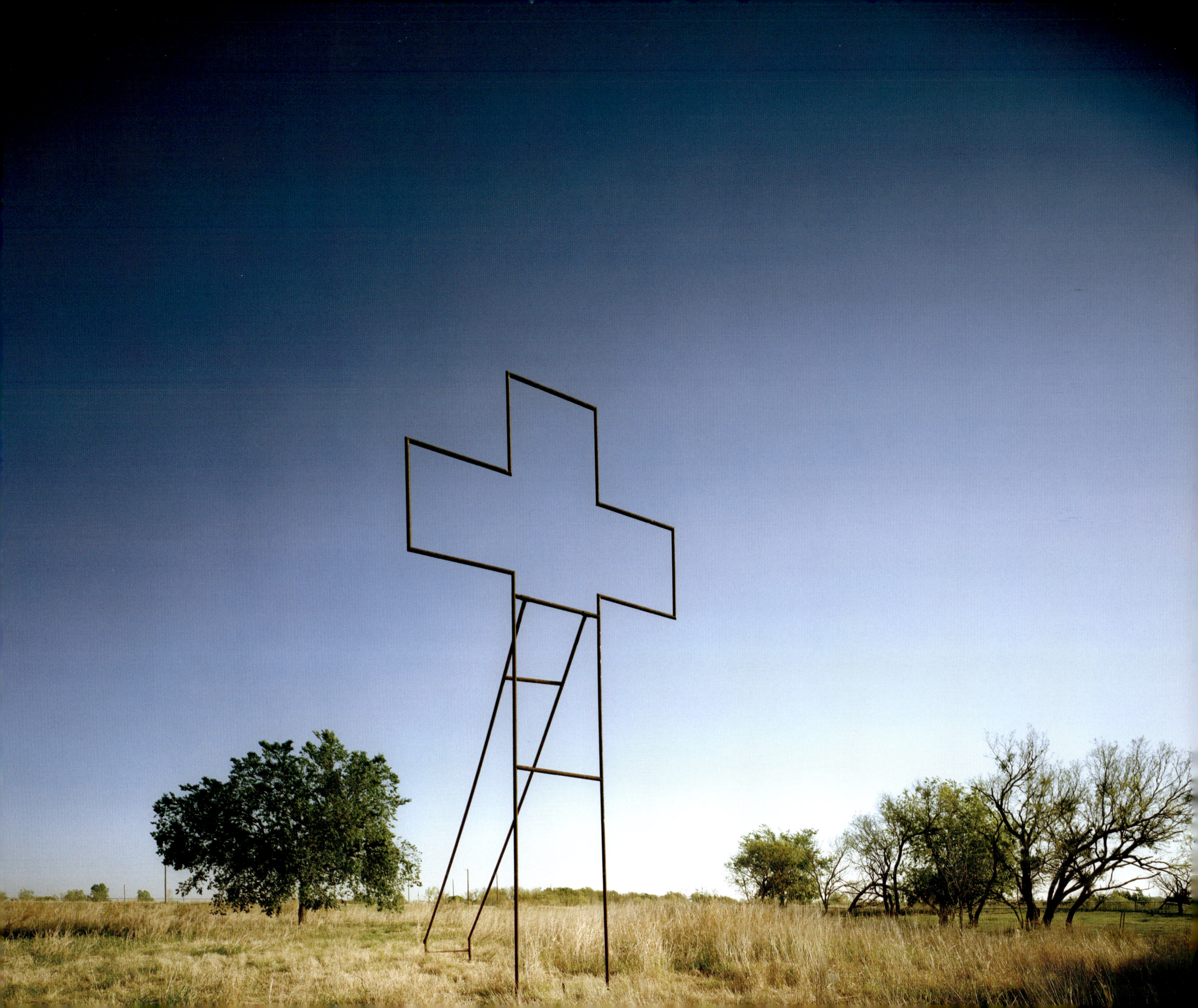

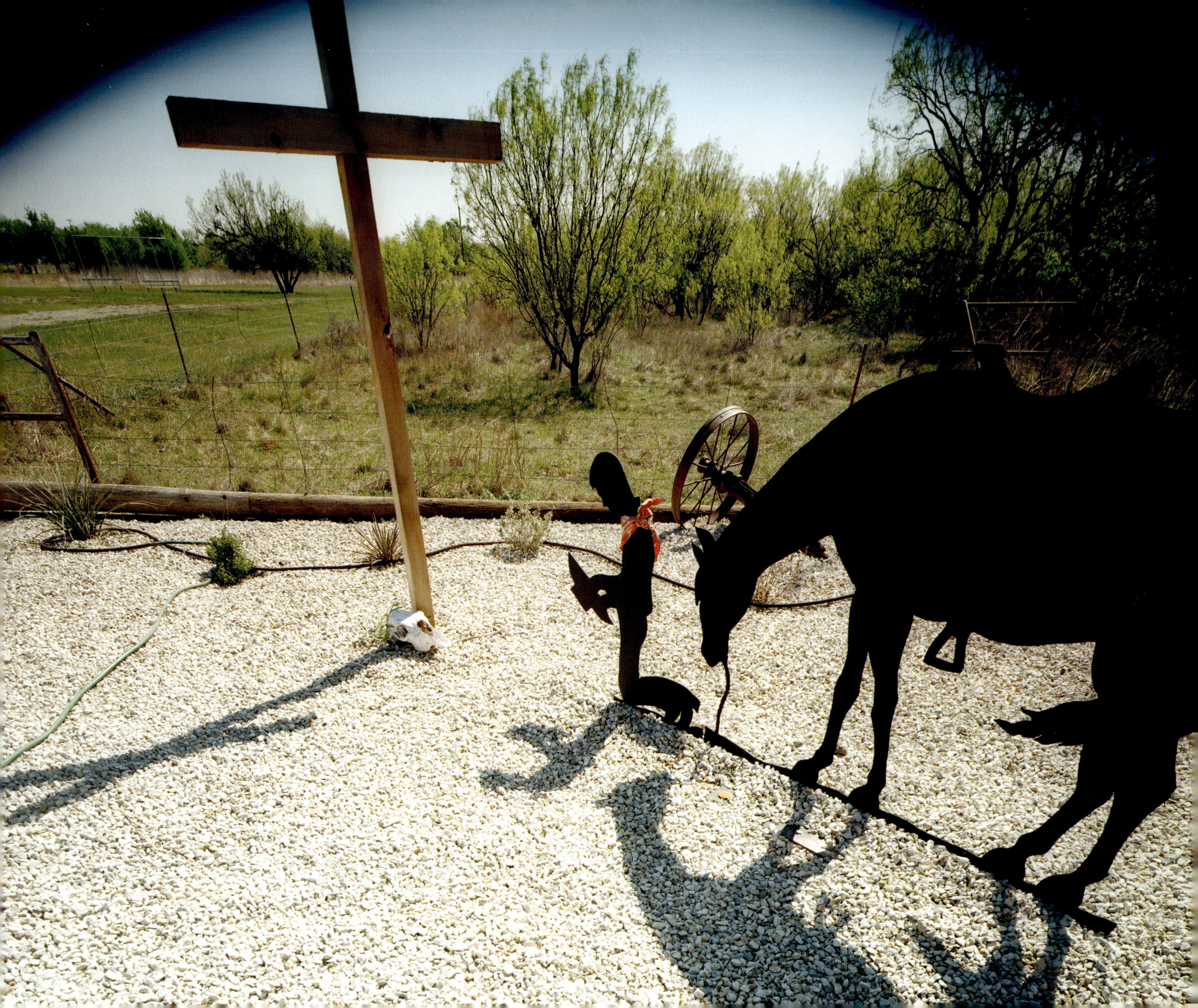

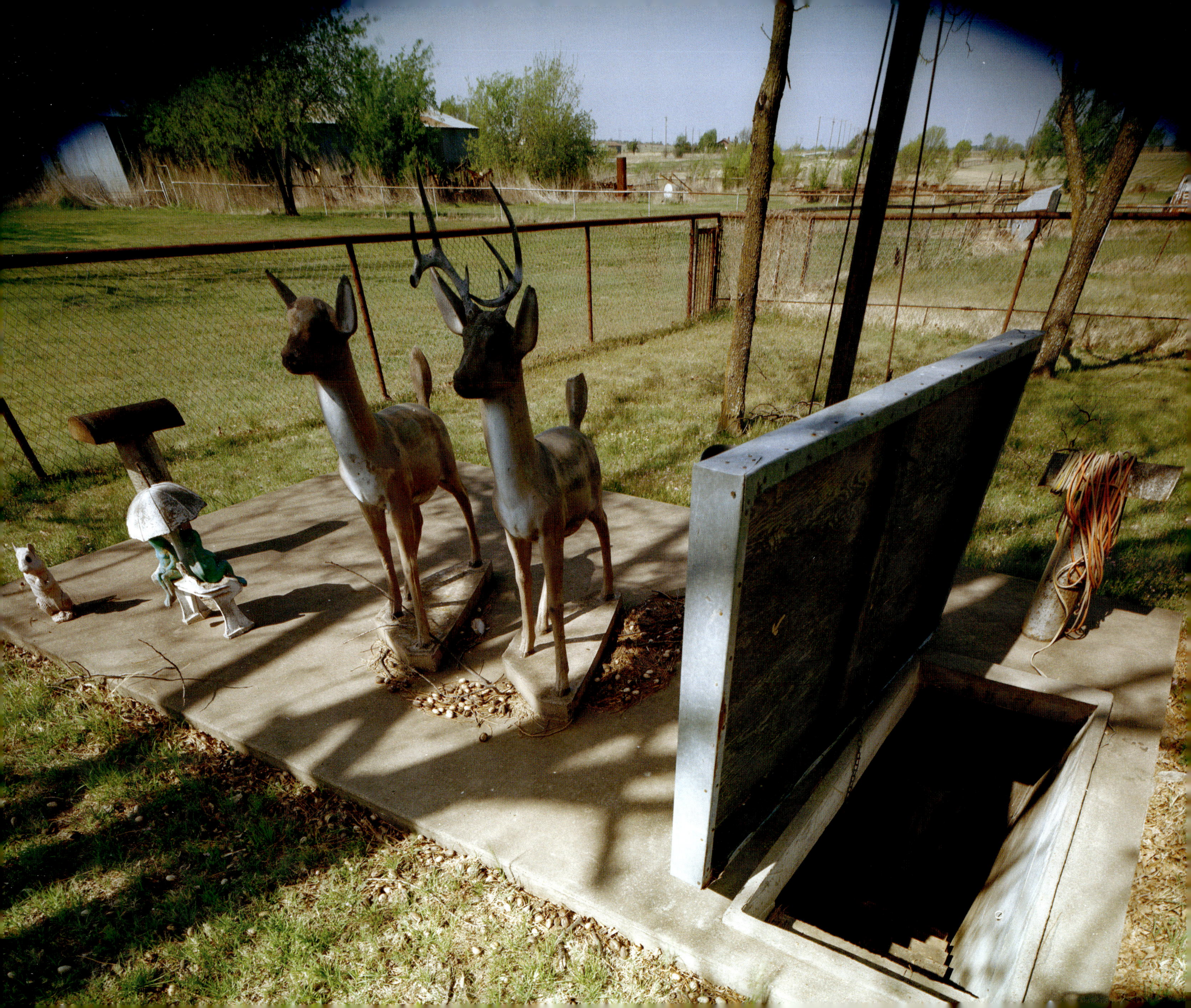

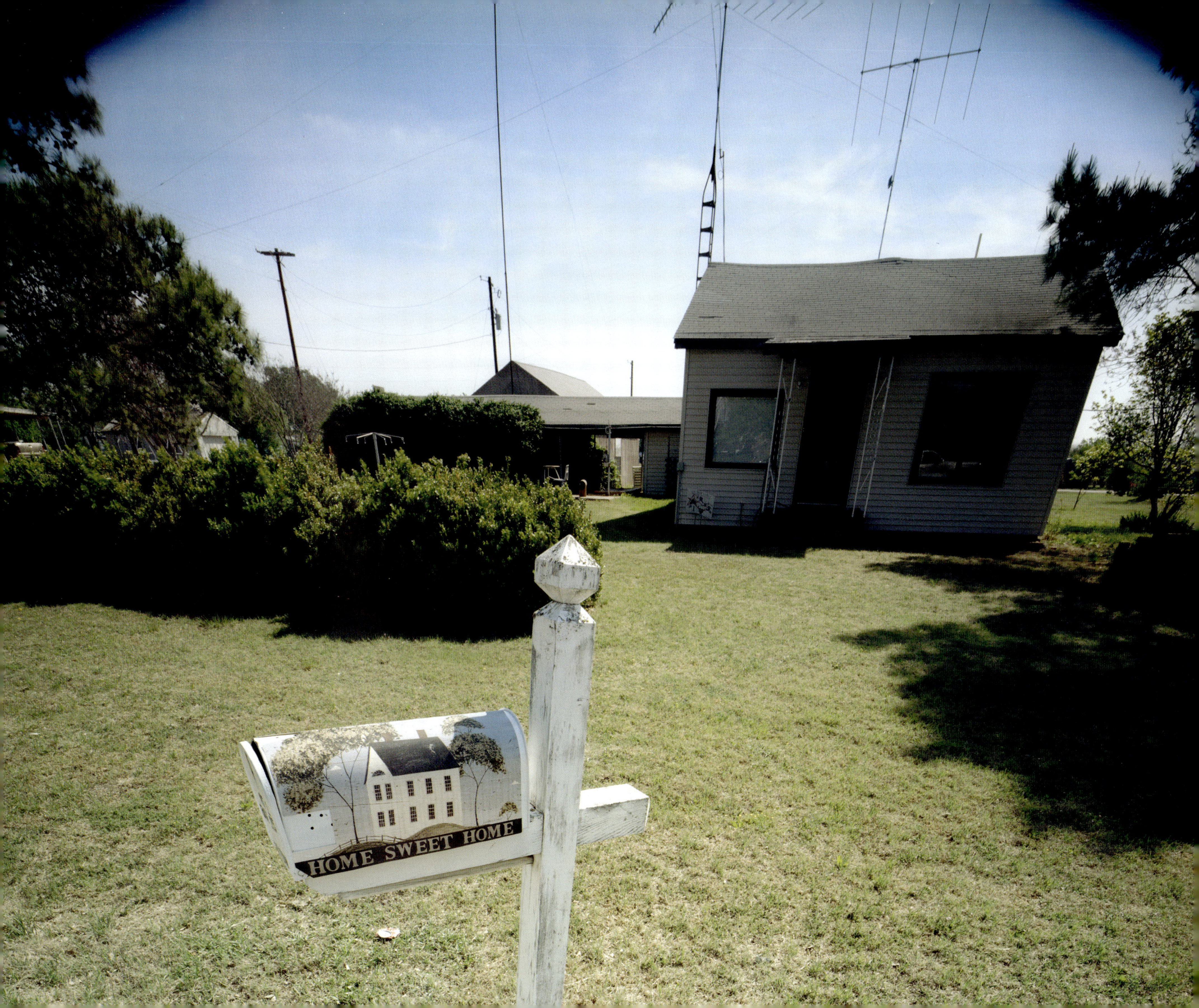
HOME SWEET HOME

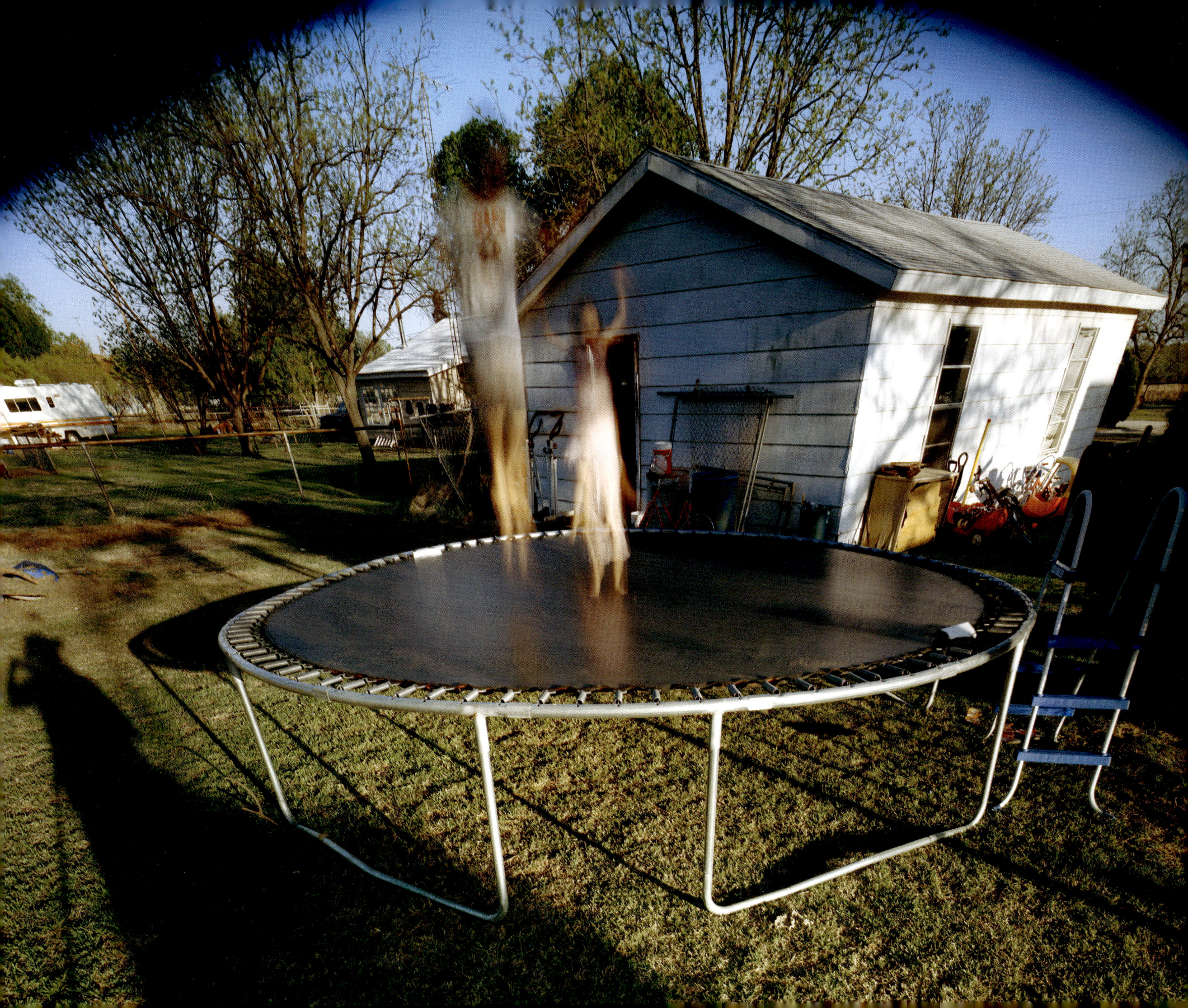

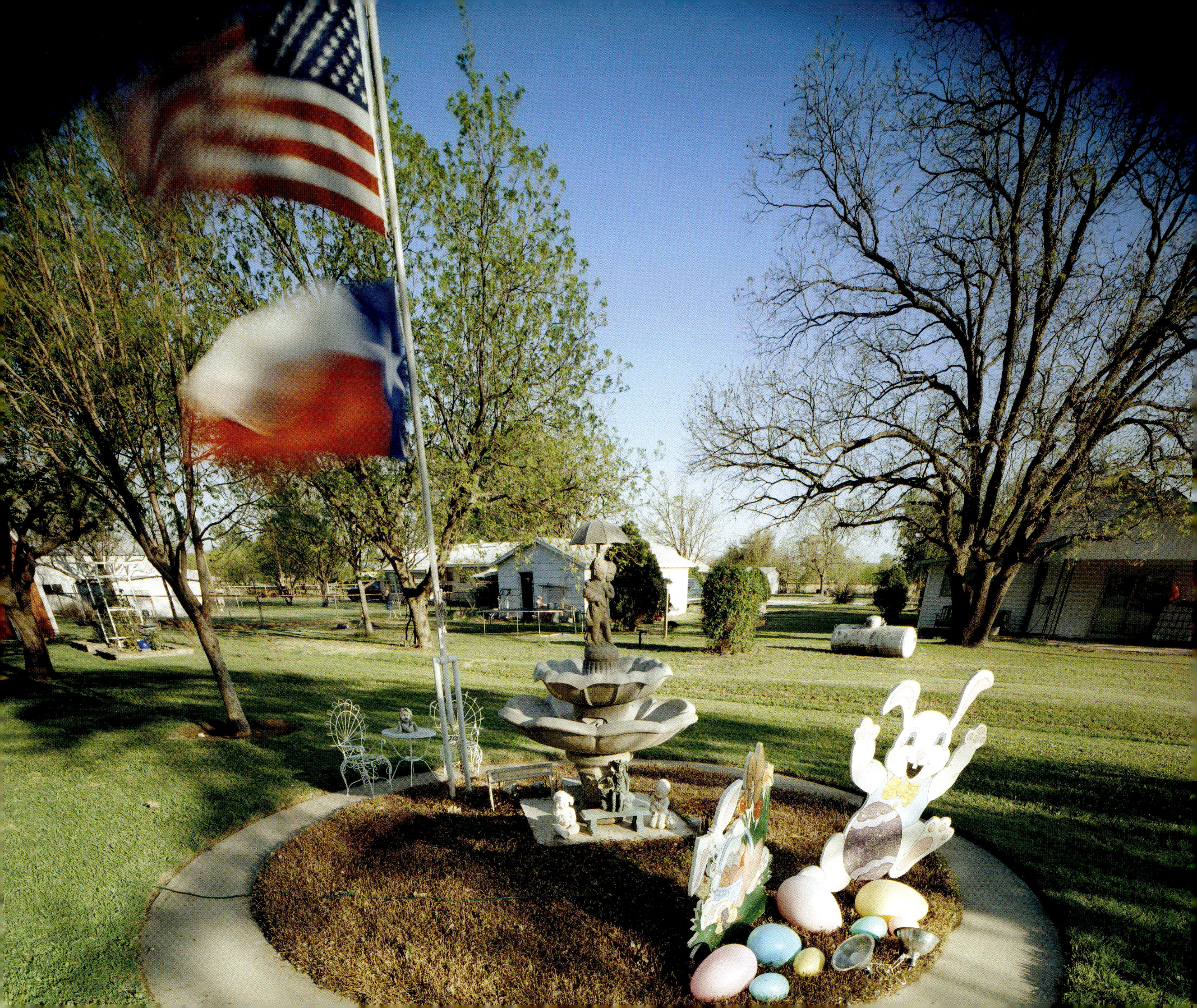

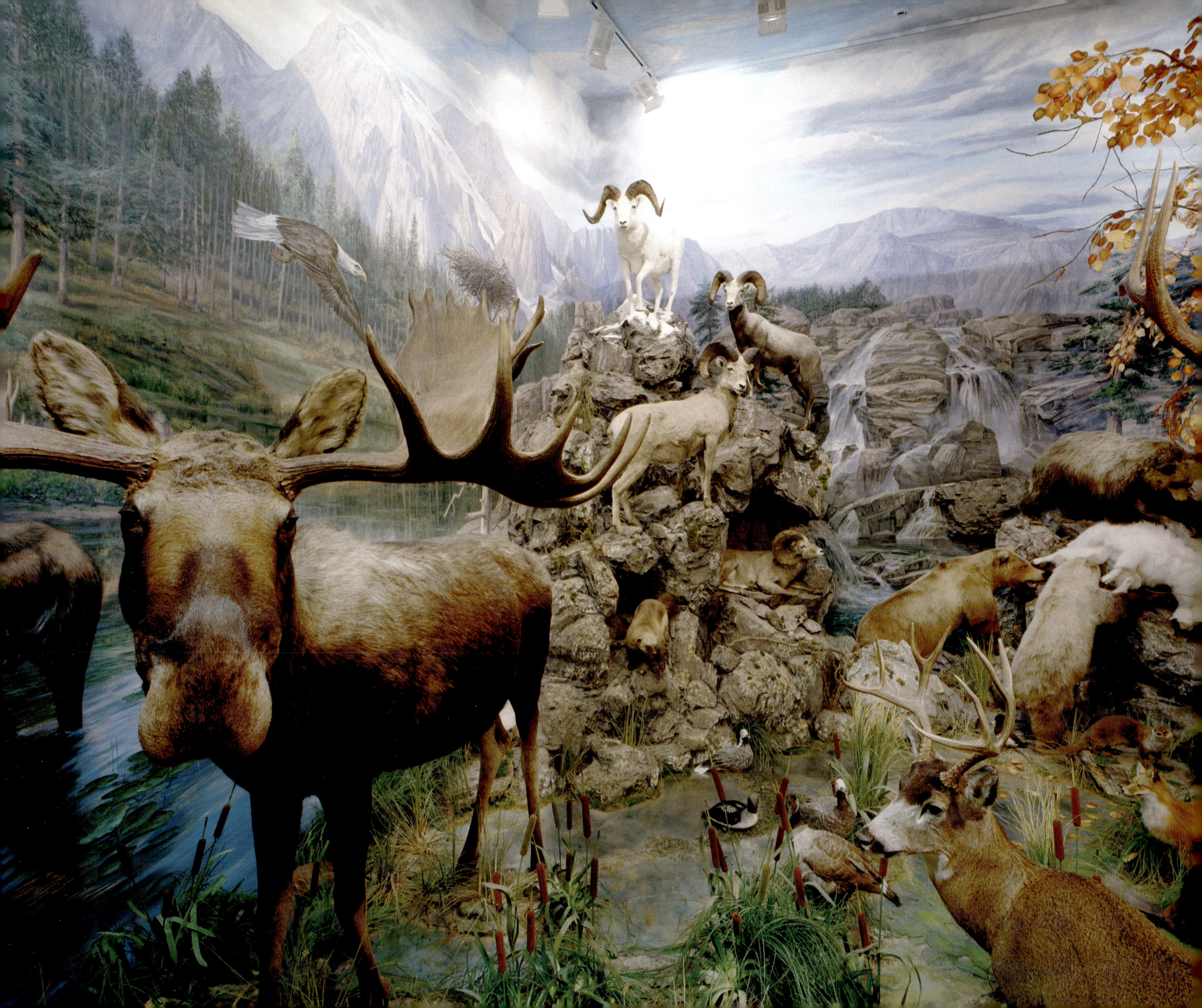

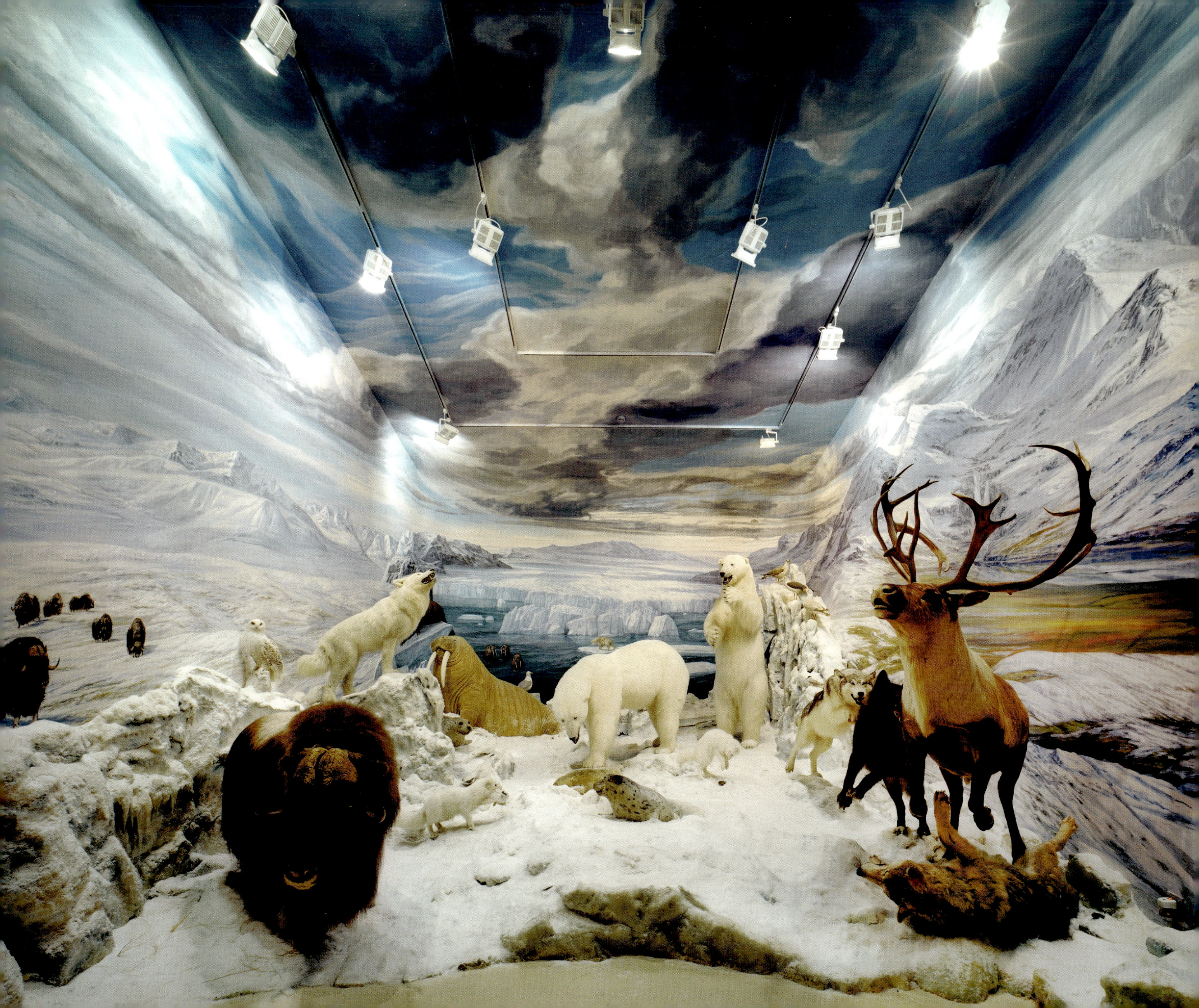

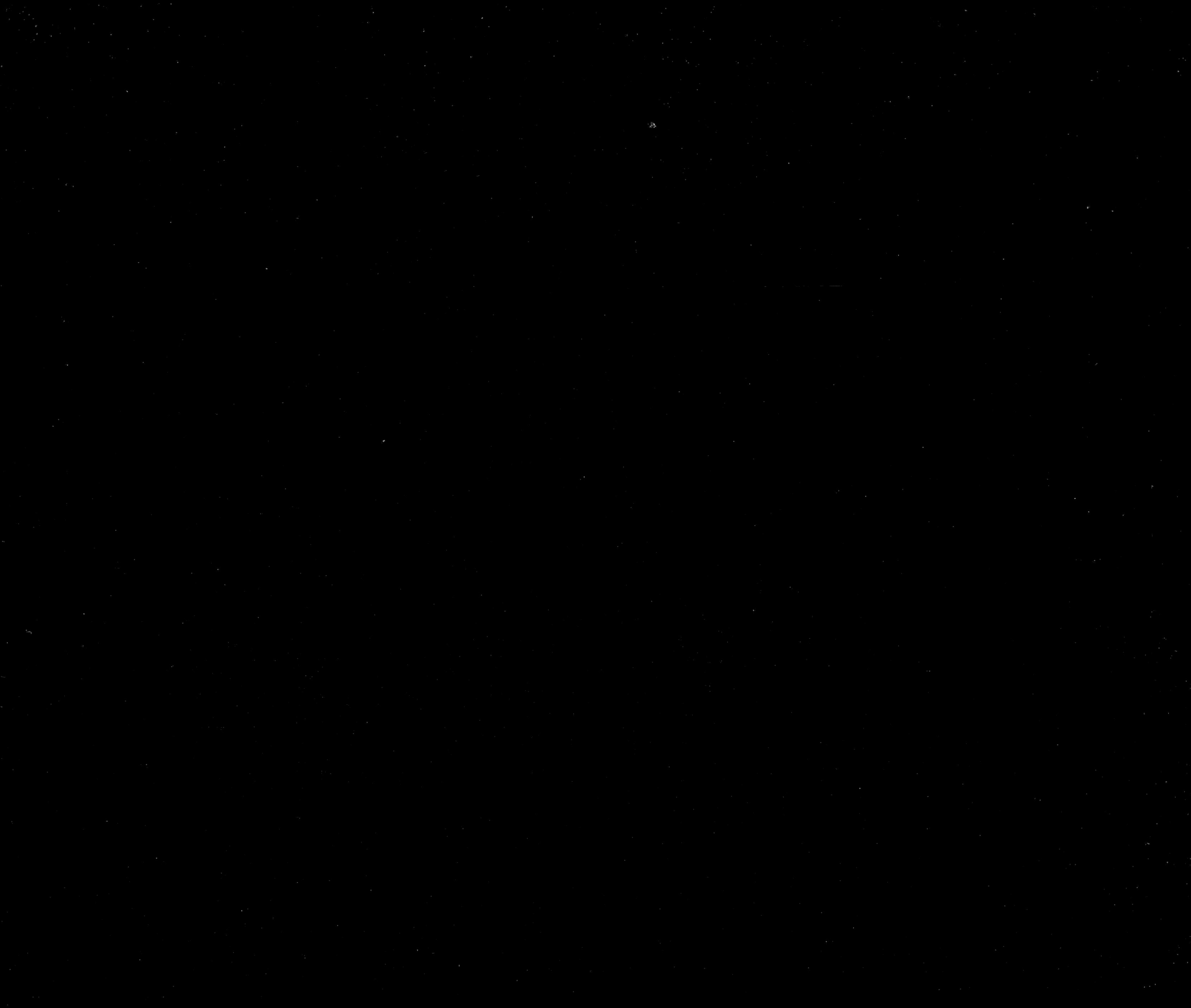

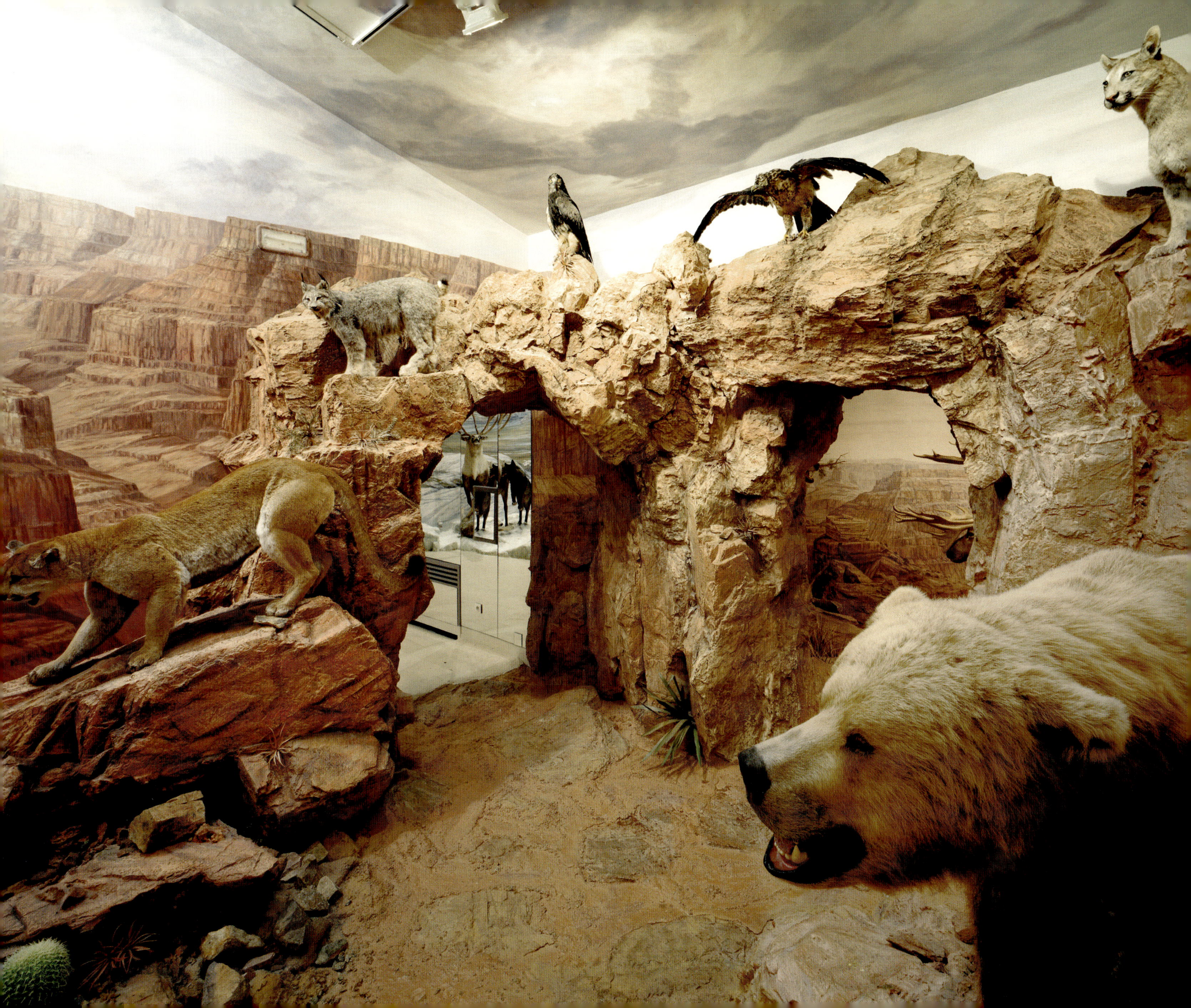

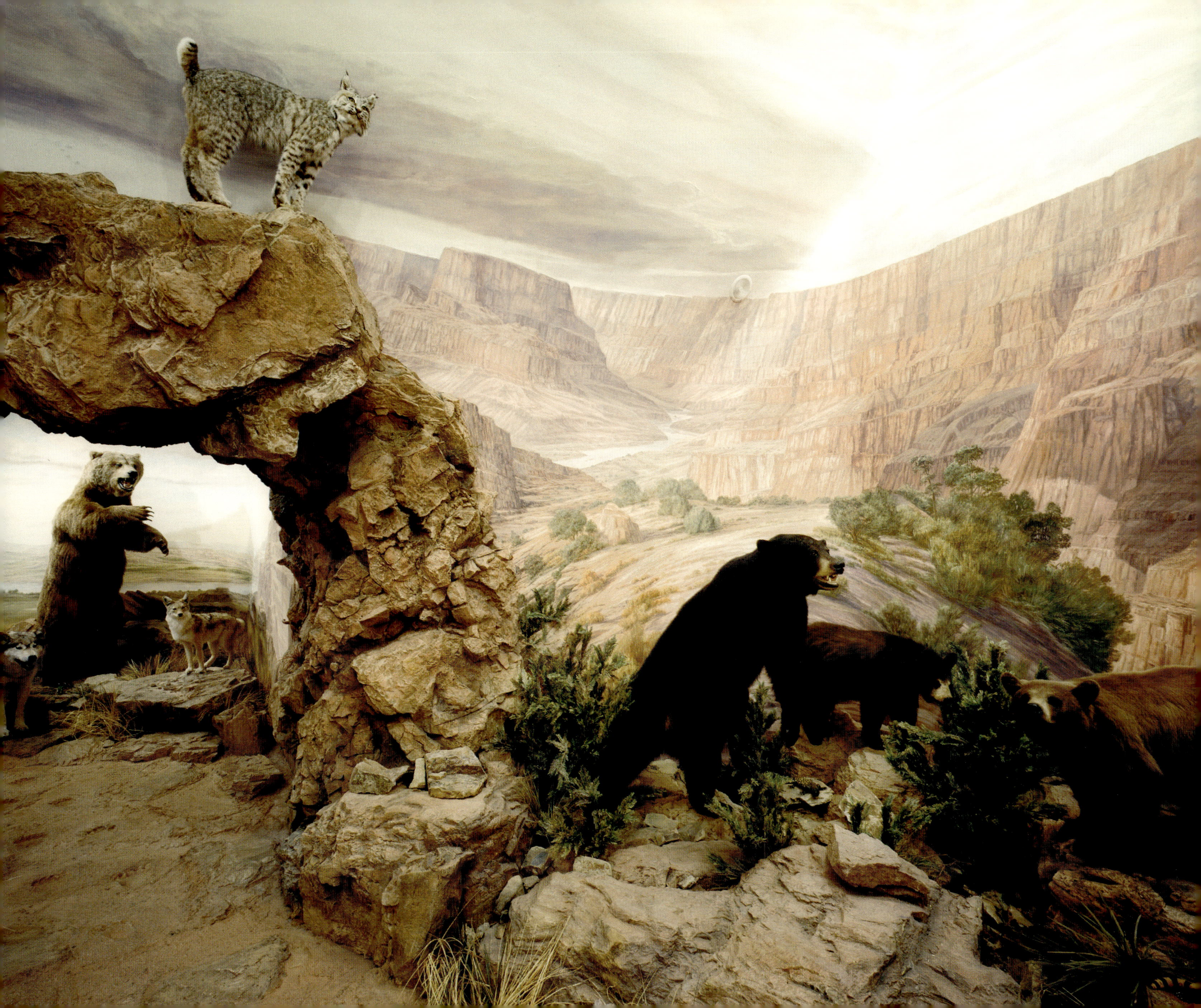

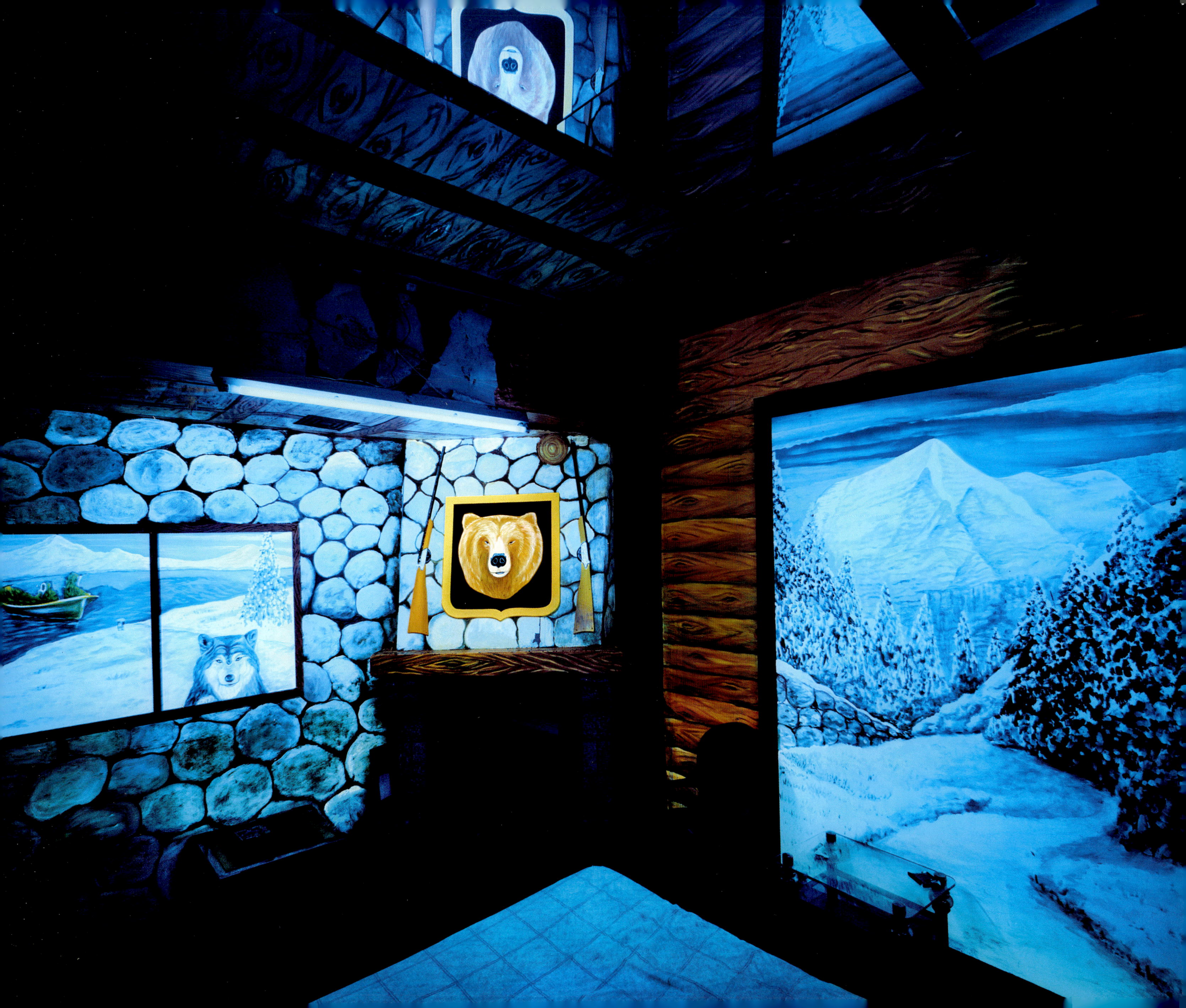

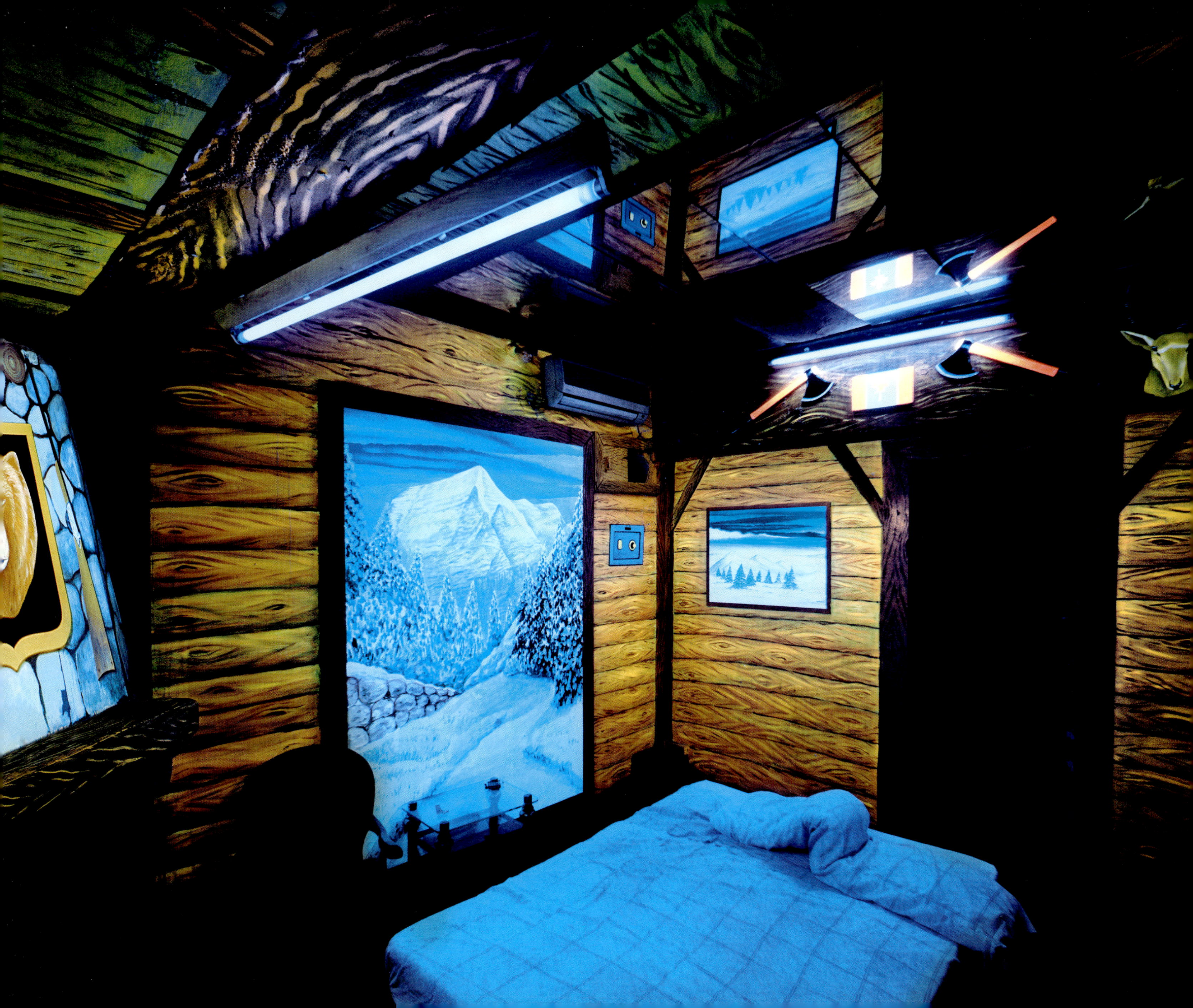

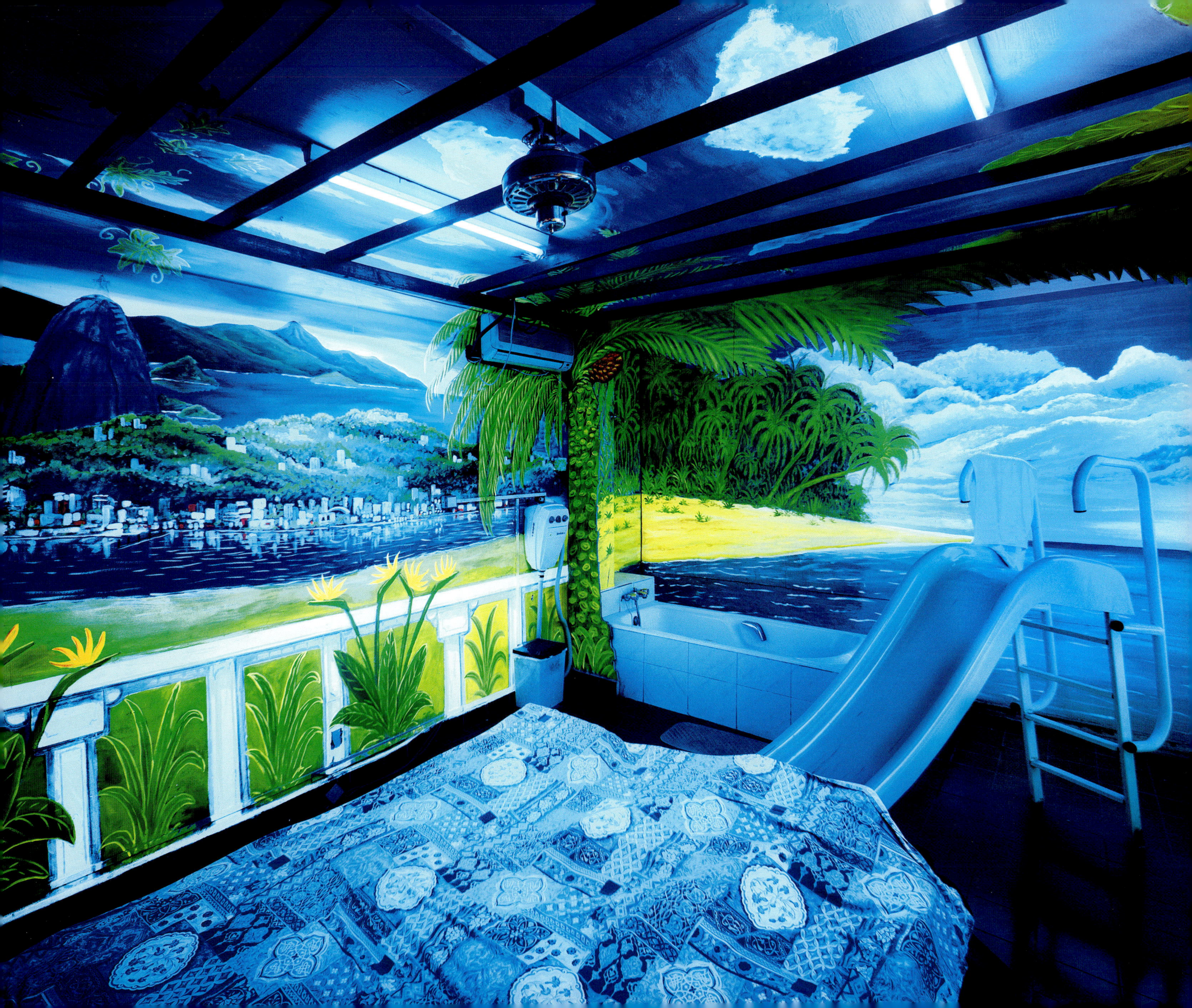

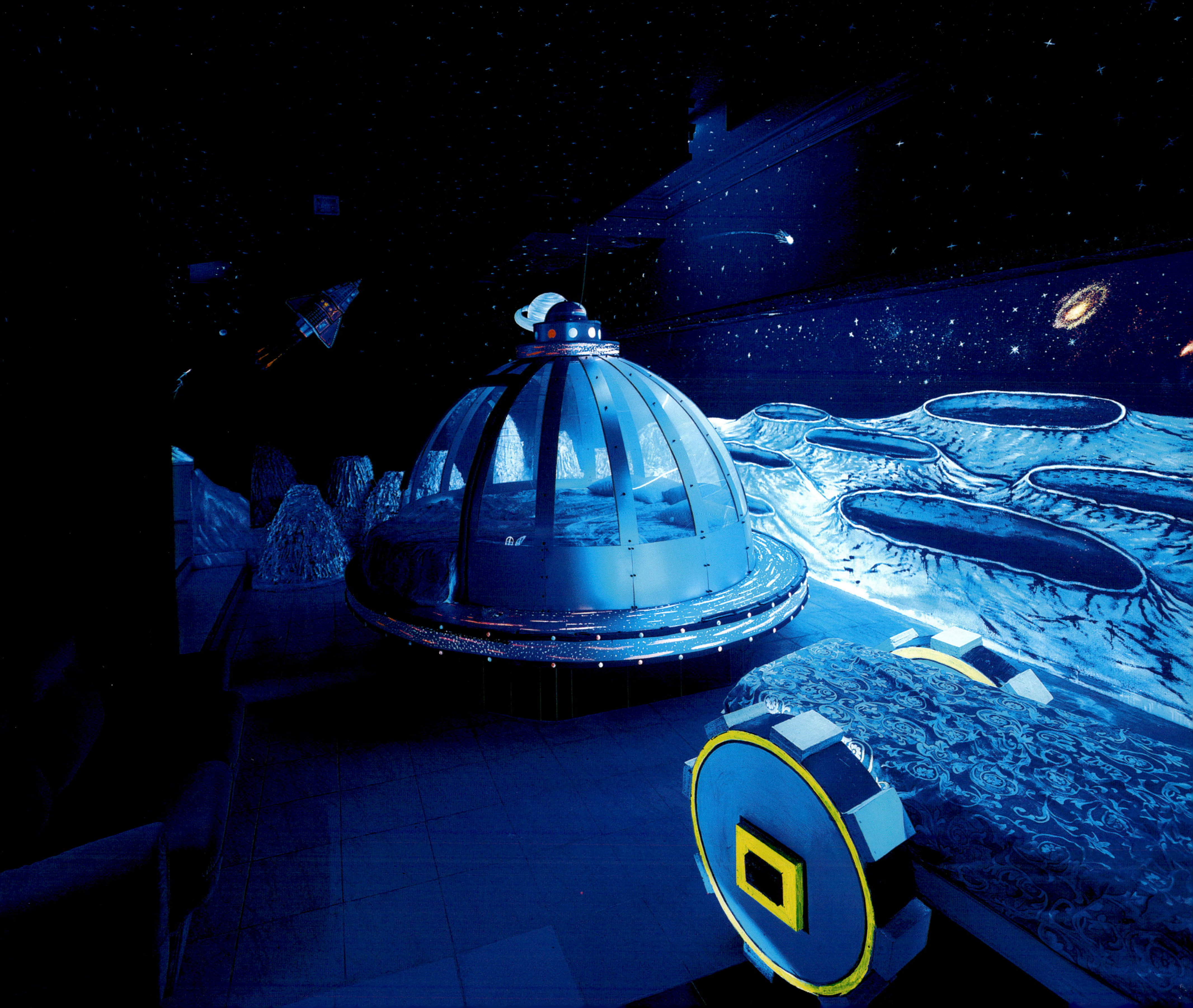

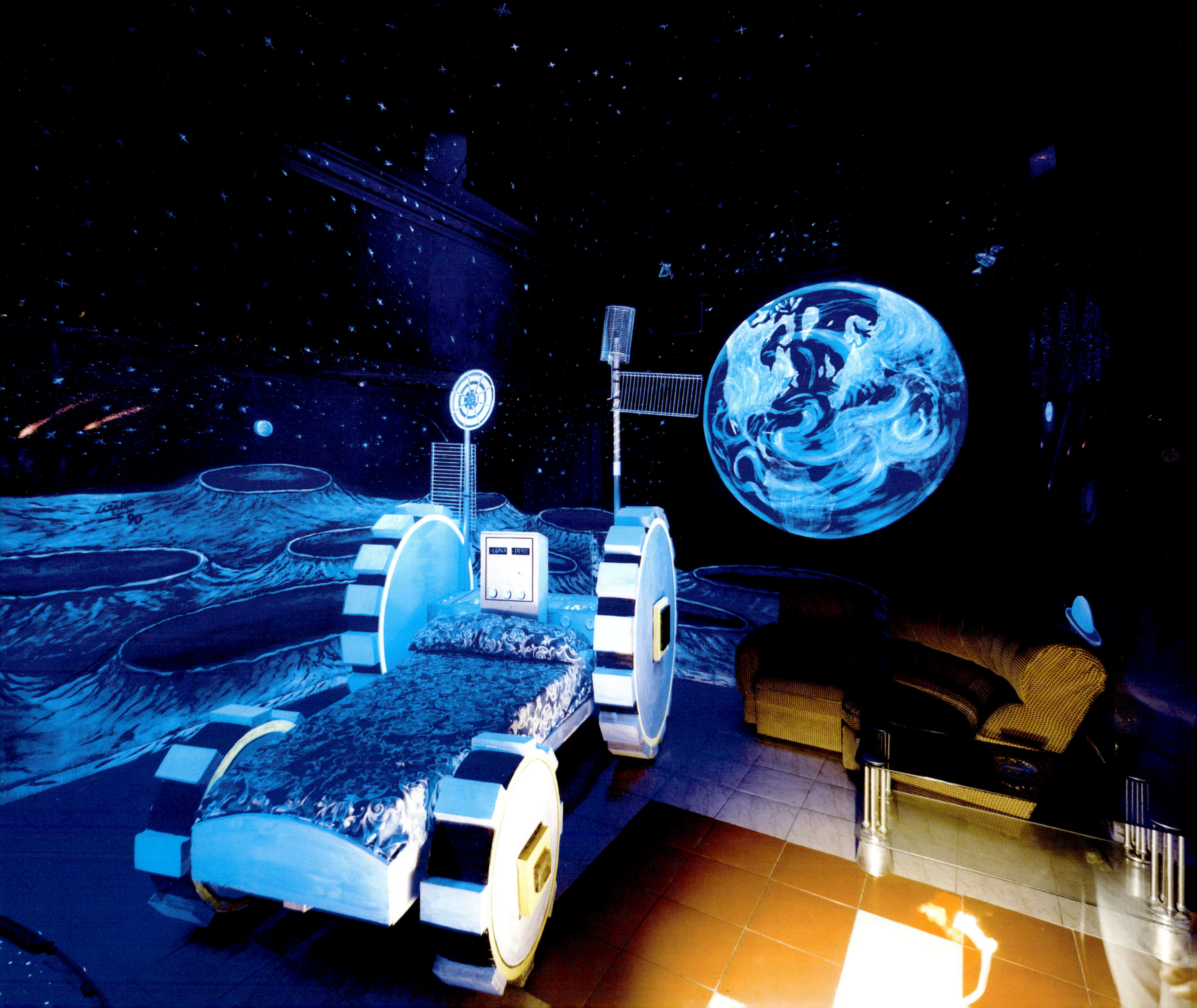

·LUNA·1990·

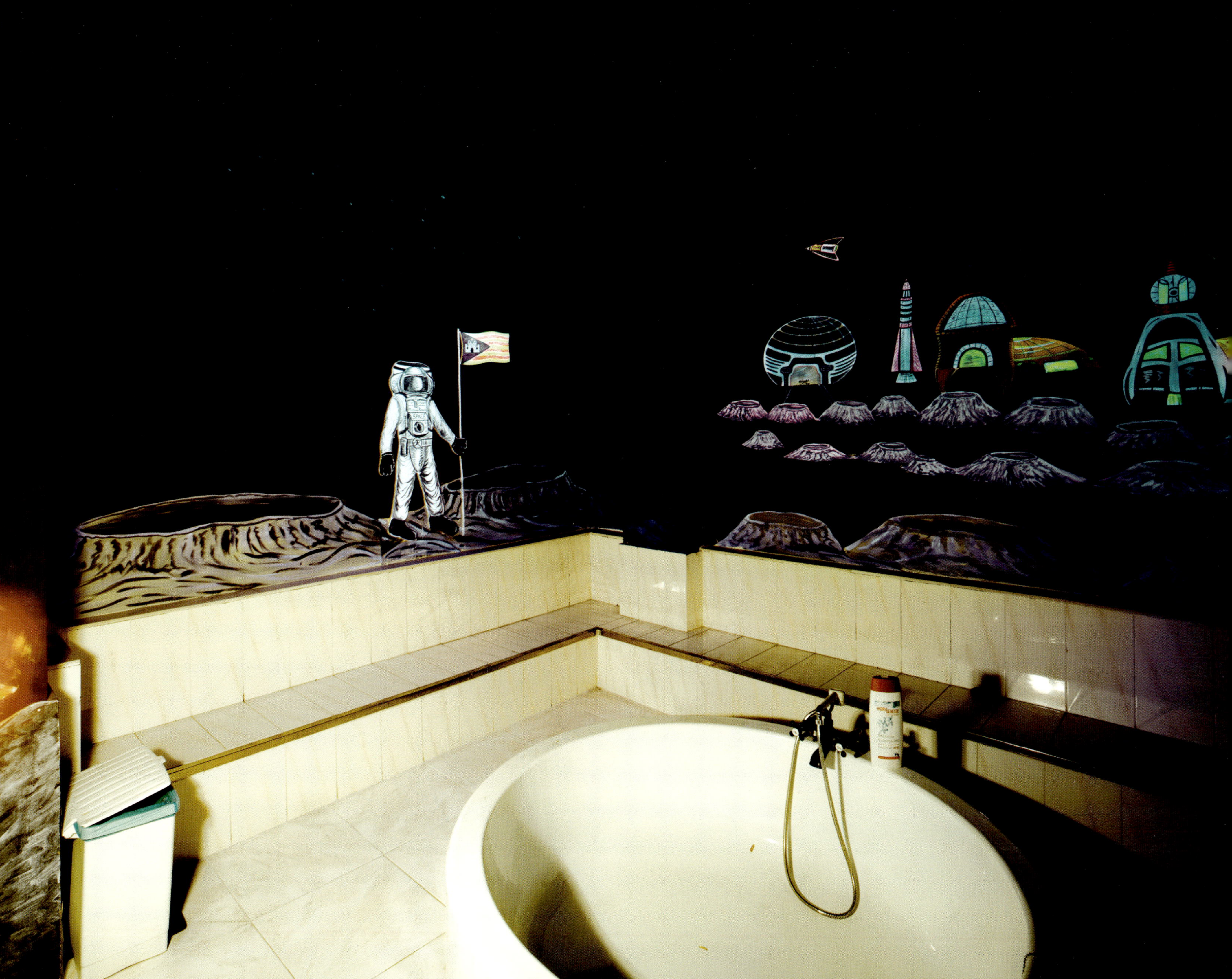

Published by
Actar
info@actar.com
www.actar.com

Photos by
Jordi Bernadó

Texts by
Adela García-Herrera
Christian Caujolle
Vicente Verdú

Graphic Design
Ramon Prat

Printed by
Ingoprint, SA

Distributed by
Actar-D
Roca i Batlle 2-4
E-08023 Barcelona
T +34 93 417 49 93
F +34 93 418 67 07
office@actar-d.com
www.actar-d.com

Actar Distribution Inc
158 Lafayette St. 5th Floor
New York, NY 10013
T +1 212 966 2207
F +1 212 966 2214
officeusa@actar-d.com
www.actar-d.com

ISBN   978-84-96540-33-0 (ang)
        978-84-96540-65-1 (cast)
DL   B-8881-2007

Printed and bound
in the European Union

Acknowledgements
Adela García-Herrera, Christian Caujolle,
Vicente Verdú , Fundació La Caixa,
Maria José Balcells, Pepa Palomar,
Anna Magre, Charles Waldheim, Miquel Molins,
Banc Sabadell, Juny Brullet, Ferran Mateo,
Jordi Fàbregas, Giacomo Delbene, Carles Puig,
Nacho Cumellas, Gloria Picazo,
Centre d'Art la Panera, Xavier Vendrell,
Pilar Marañón, Mercedes Fernández-Fuentes,
Hotel Casa Isaítas (Fuerteventura),
Klaus Berends, Vlady Nodzak Kus,
Cafetería El Naufragio (Fuerteventura),
Jorge Jordán, Familia Jordán,
residents of Loving, Jake & Sandy Paramore,
Virginia F.H Green & Fred Harrell,
Marney J. Ignacio, Club Mustang Ranch,
Bruno Pachini, Maura Pachini,
Giordano Cameli, Wendy Cameli,
Lucia Gabbani, Amalia Gabbani,
Stefano Marmusi, Marco Andrenacci,
Polígono di tiro "Le Casermette" (Cecina),
Ceramiche D'Aria (Cecina), Rafael Doctor,
MUSAC, Fundación Dr. Romero Nieto-
Museo de la Fauna Salvaje (Valdehuesa-Boñar, León),
Emiliano Armani, Generalitat de Catalunya-
Entitat Autònoma de la Difusió Cultural,
Galeria Senda, Pepita Tarragona,
Josep Bernadó, Berta Cervantes,
Actar Team, Ramon Prat, Anna Giró,
Roberto Feijoo y Giovanna Carnevali.